love & gaia

BOOKS BY CHRISTINA STRIGAS

POETRY

Your Ink On My Soul

In My Own Flood

Love & Vodka

A Book of Chrissyisms

Love & Metaxa

for all the lonely hearts being pulled out of the ground

NOVELS

Crush

The Wanting

Althia's Calling

Althia's Journey

Althia's Awakening

love & gaia

poems

Christina Strigas

love & gaia

Copyright © Christina Strigas, 2023

ISBN 978-0-9951865-9-0 Paperback

All rights reserved under International Copyright Conventions for the Protection of Literary and Artistic Works. No part of this publication may be reproduced, stored in retrieval system, transmited in any form or by any means, electronic, photocopying, printing, recording, online or otherwise without prior permission of the publisher.

Cover art by Cynthia De Gregorio

I dedicate this book to Gaia.

May she continue to heal with our love.

love & gaia

poems

Christina Strigas

CONTENTS

Introduction 1

PART I - TREES

    Vines .. 13

    Tree of Knowledge .. 16

    Orange Leaves.. 20

    My Walk ..23

    Trees ..26

    Maple..27

    Acorn ..29

    Apple Tree ..31

    Orange Tree ..34 Lemon Tree ..36

    Prune ..38 Evergreen..40

    Sycamore ..42

    Oak .. 44

PART II - SKY

    Flash ..49

    Full Moon, July 13, 2022 ..52

    The Chirp ..54

    Atmosphere ..58

    Outer Space ..59

    Sun ..61

    Moon ..63

    Planets ..65

    Stars ..67

    Constellations ..69

    Daytime Sky ..70

    Night Sky ..72

    Clouds ..74

    Rainbows ..76

    Smog ..78

    Pollution ..79

    Kites ..81

PART III - OCEAN

    The Sea Also Rises ..85

    Waves ..89

    Shore ..90

    Ionian ..92

    Aegean ..94

    River ..96

    Lake ..98

    Shells ..100

    Pebbles ..102

    Pacific ..104

    Sea of Atlas ..106

    Water ..108

    Blue ..110

    Splash ..112

    Animals in the Ocean ..113

    Dock ..115

PART IV - SOIL

    Earth ..119

    Dirt ..120

    Solids ..121

    Liquids ..122

    Gases ..126

    Minerals ..128

    Organisms ..130

    Organic Matter ..132

PART V - TEA LEAVES

    Tea Leaves ..138

    Green Tea ..141

    Sage ..143

    Color ..145

    Your Future ..148

    Cloves .. 152

    Cinnamon Bark ..154

    Chamomile ..155

    Vervain ..157

Cretan Herbs ..158

Turmeric ..159

PART VI - COFFEE BEANS

Blend ..163

Whole ..164

Espresso ..165

Gold-Leaf Royal Albert ..166

Giving You Up ..167

Grains ..170

Coffeehouse ..172

Instant ..175

Organic ..177

Our First Meeting ..179

PART VII - HERBS

Coriander ..183

Mint ..184

Dill ..186

Lavender ..188

Rosemary ..189

Italian Basilisc ..191

Greek Basil ..194

PART - VIII - SEEDS

Choke ..199

Plant ..201

Petal ..206

Stem ..209

Leaves ..212

Flowers ..214

Soil Below My Feet ..216

PART IX -GAIA

My Skin is Green and Blue ..221

The Shift of a Historical area ..225

In the Past ..228

Panda ..234

Yanomami Woman ..237

Reminders of Nature ..248

Space X .. 239

PART X - LOVE

Love ..243

PART XI - UNIVERSE

energy ..269

air ..270

fire ..271

water ..272

earth ..274

universe ..275

Part XII – ENERGY

Between Us ..279

Snow ..281

I Like Lonely People ..284

Ode to the Landfill ..286

The Nature of her Hands ..289

One Among Many ..291

Six Stones from a Beach ..294

No ..300

The Bike Path ..303

PART XIII – HABITATS

Mojave Desert ..309

The Amazon ..311

Polar ..315

Tundra ..317

Evergreen Forests ..320

Seasonal Forests ..323

Grasslands ..324

Thalassa ..326

Reiki ..327

Facts ..329

A Story ..330

Solar Energy ..334

Dear Gaia ..337

Rotations of the Earth ..342

Revolution ..344

Love Letters ..346

Birthday ..349

Radioactive Decay ..351

In Sickness ..353

Miracles ..354

Part XIV – INTERNAL EARTHQUAKES

EPILOGUE ACKNOWLEDGMENTS

IMAGE CREDITS

ABOUT THE AUTHOR

INTRODUCTION

Sept. 23, 2022

As I lay in bed after meditating, the room swirled in hues of purple and gold. This made me think of an array of poems. I thought of an idea for a new poetry book, but with no toxins involved. This would be a first for me.

It would be a spiritual poetry book.

The other day, I walked into a supermarket that is near my house. I would walk to it throughout the years to get any food I ran out of, but on that particular day, the smell in the aisles made me almost gag. It smelled like rotting meat and death. I left immediately and vowed not to go back.

Once you let in the light of the universe, your soul will tell you where to go.

Now, there is a new owner, and the smell is gone. It's a new version with a fresh scent. I get my fresh rapini and grapes from there. We can let old narratives go.

I thought of a title for my poetry book, Love & Tea, and I immediately messaged Lex. She's always the first person I tell my ideas to. It was 6:30 am; I was barely awake. She said it's "too basic. Think of something that rhymes with Metaxa and vodka."

This is our text conversation:

Me: *Gm, I got a thought to write another book Love & Tea or Love & Coffee & Tea and this book will have more nature poems and the ones I wrote about the trees, etc and write an entire book on nature and not love and erotica*

What do you think?

More of a spiritual book

Poetry book

And it ends the "trilogy"

"Lol"

Lex: *I like it but maybe tweaked like love & tea leaves or idk*

Something that isn't

love coffee tea lol

Me: *Yes*

Good idea

I like that

Tea leaves

Lex: *There's a lot of different magical words that are not so concrete and used 24/7*

Me: *Yes*

True

Lex: *Plus you can see the future with T leaves right*

Me: *Sage*

Yes

Tea leaves

I like that a lot

You're right

Lex: *Yeah that sounds good but bet there's other good ones too*

Me: *I will use tea leaves for now*

Lex: *Is there something that kind of rhymes with vodka*

Metaxa vodka

Hmmmm

Lex: *Chocolate*

Lmao

Me: *Lmao*

Herbs

Lol

I have to think

Seeds

Lex: *I'm good with odd and slant rhymes I'll think about it*

Me: *Ok*

(heart emoji)

Lex: *Love & latkes (laughing emojis)*

Me: *Hahaha*

Lex: *Is potato pancakes*

I love those

Me: *Me2*

I used to make them with my prek class

Lex: *Love & Prada*

Laughing emoji

Me: *Love & Honey*

Lex: *Nooooo*

Me: *Never*

Lol

Jk

Lex: *Love & Tilapia*

Me: *Love & Earth*

Lex: *All mine rhyme*

With metaxa vodka

Me: *Let me think*

Lex: *Love & Erotica*

Laughing emoji

I like tilapia

Me: *I can't think*

I need to get up

Wash up and think

I really am blank with words that rhyme with that

Love & Gaia

I got it

It came to me

I love it

What do you think?

Lex: *Yeah*

Perfect!!!!

Me: *(White heart emoji)*

Lex: *You could have sections like tea leaves*

Me: *Exactly*

The trees

The earth

Etc

Lex: *Space X poem*

Me: *Tea leaves*

Earth blah

Lex: *Sections*

Me: *Yes*

I never had a title before a book

Lex: *Yeah it's a cool idea*

Me: *Lol*

It came to me when I meditated

(heart emoji)

Thank you

For the rhyme idea!

Lex: *(red heart emoji)*

I

Trees

PART I

———————

TREES

VINES

Listen to the language of the trees

read their bark

kiss their vines

sit under their branches

read a book of poetry

close your tired eyes

give it an honest hug

do not look around

to see if anyone is looking

be a child

stop caring

embrace your inner child

tell that child

your truth

Take a walk together in a family of trees

tell each other

how families have roots

inside our skin

Listen to the language of the trees

they speak in silence

learn that alphabet.

TREE OF KNOWLEDGE

In my center
>lies my eye that people see

as they place a blanket under me deep
within are a thousand more eyes

that few can see above peach skies I
crack a nut and wait for you
>but my branches are so true

alive with written texts in obscure languages
of the past. We outlive time and remain last.

Dear humans,

>I am weary, strong. I have my source of energy,

but you walk or drive by me as if I am a homeless person.
My sign reads
>*stop, look, sit, talk, touch me*

but you cannot read my language anymore.

I was once loved very much and also taken advantage of
many times. Fooled by trust. My family was removed, cut
down. I still hear the echo of silence. My cousin's arms
connected to mine. We were together for over four
hundred years. I heard some humans and their machines
coming closer, but we could not run. We are not meant to
hide. In silence, we teach. We are not meant to be cut for
greed, but our mother seeks karma now. It is karma

humans brought upon themselves by making more out of us and wanting more of our minds. We are the tables and chairs in your house. We are in your cupboards, on your decks. Families, we hold up your roof. Our roots protect you. We hold up your string beans, tomatoes, and make your roses grow straight. We are on your shoes, on your kitchen table, we mix your salad. All the parts of us you drive by are near you daily. You refuse to notice us because you like your pretty things and objects, but our knowledge is not temporary.

   We are leaves of every shape you drew as kids. In natural symmetry, we come in hearts, in diamonds, in squares, in triangles, in circles. We come in peace, while you continue to hunt us, defy law, break our eyes apart, and still you cannot read our minds. You think we have none? You cannot trust our instincts. You think it does not exist. You cannot look into our eyes. You do not see any.

With Love,

The Tree of Knowledge

speaking on behalf of all trees

ORANGE LEAVES

The colors are more orange-red

than yellow. On TV everything looks

controlled, in reality, it's chaos.

Change is gonna come are lyrics to

a song redone over and over again

but the tint of hatred is red

heat and black smoke. I smell

the soot, the ash. My eyes

hurt me, but it is mostly my

heart that keeps tugging

over the burning of the soil,

trees, leaves, branches. They

crackle and create a

funeral tune. No one on my

right, no one on my left.

I wonder where all the

humans hide when in

terror. Do they slide into

bunks? Do they drive

to the end of the earth

only to find no dead end

truly exists.

  I walk toward the heat

like a woman with no labels

none of the culture wars

matter on this edge. You

burn or live a new life

with the known fact

you can only look forward

into the future

and let the experiment

come to its sad final blow.

Let the onyx hearts win

once again as the flames

rise, turn the magenta sky

gray, isolated.

I see no more sun, no more moon

only ethereal words on paper

up in red flames

the night takes over the day

as my last breath

becomes ashes on a shore.

MY WALK

Once I saw a bunny hopping.

I can see through the sadness

of the photos full of smiles.

Being a writer is a battle

with words and silence.

I walk everywhere now

I prefer it to the gym

people exasperate me

and this poem is about

one thing, and everything

except you.

I promised Lex: no men, no sex,

yet you text me

and I am distracted

it's the concrete and how it eats up

the eyes of the trees

the way you eat up my soul

with melancholic illusion

and I fill my tea with ginger and basil.

I see this low-spirited building

it's gray and black

ultra-modern chic

with four glass balconies

two have patio tables

and the other two are empty slabs of concrete

that surround the peppered gravel

the garage door is a wild cage

as I recall the bunny that hopped here

when I was ten years old

and then I get a flash of my grandfather walking me

to school every morning

I look at the balcony with the yellow cushions

and two white chairs

that was where I saw the cardinal bird

in this timeline

no one knows what hides inside buildings

the sunlight of the forest

keeps disappearing into brick and mortar

a slow death of vibrant life

I don't know why I'm crying again

Is it the forest dying from lack of love

or me?

TREES

One fell to my foot

with a tinge of red unmatched in any dye

no matter how hard you may try

One is on my lawn

yellow — a shade lighter than the sun

keeping me on a constant run

One is in your eyes —

a green I memorized from birth

to make all your glances more than one worth

One is in your eyes

the sparks of green

that shows me all you've seen.

None of these leaves are about you

yet all of them are.

MAPLE

I made pancakes for him

an oatmeal energy ball

with a touch of your love

sprinkled oats on you

some flax seeds

chia seeds

natural peanut butter

I went to *cabane a sucre*

sugaring off

listened to the Indigenous tales

of how they discovered you

by accident

a natural accident

to supply us with

so many sweet family gatherings

I pour you into my heart

with a dash of brown sugar

to lessen the heartache.

You have cured me

of my loneliness

on so many barren days

and your season

is the one

I recall

the most

from childhood

licking your *tige*

from Popsicle sticks

in the middle of a forest

of fallen leaves.

ACORN

Collected your droppings

to make some art

with my class

one year we painted

your edges white

put a ribbon on you

sprinkled some glitter

and added you

to our Christmas tree

packaged you up

as a gift

to cherish every year.

Another year

we painted

your edges

added silver glitter

made them

come alive

with summer colors

but your fall

will never be covered up

you keep reminding us

of your existence

every time we walk.

APPLE TREE

Jazz Autumn colors

twist inside this room

one piano melody

and your freedom lifts.

Stand nearby

and watch how

we pick

apple trees —

no, do not pull

delicately twist the stem

sing from your core

let the seeds sit inside

your stomach

sprout strength

one green apple a day

fights more evil

than a war field

let the natural taste

of sweet and sour

linger on your lips

let the children

pick their two-pound bags

eat a few

throw half away

spit out the pips

smell the moment

hug a parent

snap

the sunlight is in their eyes.

When you look at the picture now

you recall how the braids on your daughter

shone with love in the sun

as she squinted up at you with her perfect smile

and two-year-old eyes.

ORANGE TREE

You can live up to one hundred years
but you prefer fiifty or sixty years
to prove your worth

I used to smell you
when I was pregnant and nauseous

You brought me back to life

I put you in my lunchbox
every day to taste your love

Your arms grow from your trunk
renew your foliage
bloom with buds
white flowers
People grow you for profit

I would grow you for love if I could

your vitamins make my skin glow at fiifty-four

you keep me strong

fight all the viruses

But most of all

I can drink you fresh

receive you fully with love

I will not go a day without you

you are more stable than any love

your taste in my mouth

explosive and safe.

LEMON TREE

At every age you create a world

with your mere presence

an existence

of scents

to place in drinks

soup, meals sweets —

a kiss between lovers

a lyric in a song you cannot forget

a walk in a backyard

where my uncle grew up in Greece

and we fell asleep

one afternoon

to wake to its aroma

a rind to place on your lips

a yellow cake with poppy seeds

a morning drink with pure water

victorious you

unforgettable you

your bitterness breaks boundaries.

PRUNE

We found you in 1976

not sure who planted you

but your lavish dark inheritance

replaced our morning strawberry jam.

The taste of you was bizarre

at first

I wondered why my mom did not

add more sugar

she only said

some foods are not meant to be sweet

I came to terms with your

unique explosion in my mouth

the pit inside

we tossed back to the earth

I sit under you at fifteen

read historical romance fiction novels

at fifteen cents a book

my dad bought me

one after the other I devour the books

with your leftover flavor

on my fingertips

We gave you as gifts

to neighbors and friends

preserved you in mason jars

you are a passenger of time

understanding a lifespan more than humans

ever could.

When we sold that house

we sold your story

we stopped making that jam

and now the store bought one

will never taste the same as you.

EVERGREEN

In her dignified stately stance

She holds your dreams on her pine

She wants you to notice her prim style

Her flushed innocence of your own youth.

You underestimate her nose in the air

For pride, but it's the complete opposite.

It's not your belief in gods she cares about

It's your belief in your own will

She used to live in the country

When cities never existed.

Her titles are fabricated

Plebian, proletarian means nothing to her

She never googles silly words

Only silence matters to her

From time to time

She sways to children singing

Christmas carols

Or playing hide and seek

In the middle of summer

She never sheds or changes her color to orange

She is the queen of the country

Graceful and notorious for her reliability.

SYCAMORE TREE

His nicknames are unknown to all

Only his close friends

Whisper silently to him

> *Hey buttonwood*
>
> *Hey butonball*

They have been next to each other

For four hundred years

Reading each other's bark

Without words

Theirs is a beautiful language of

S I L E N C E

Their thoughts on humanity

Bring forth

All the shame you disguise as

Happiness.

He is eight feet tall

Looks at how you

Stare out the window

Without seeing him.

His humility is solid

You leave your window open

For the fresh air

He knows you are unaware

Unconscious of his part

In your daily breath

And he forgives you.

OAK TREE

Insects live inside my house

Oxygen is produced by my very being

Squirrels collect my acorns

And I come in white, red, and black.

You bought my buffet

At the antique store in 1996

The year you got married

For seven hundred dollars

You hold onto my lion legs

And red velvet drawers

But no one else loves me

Like you do

They give me away to the poor

They say I am too old now

As if I have an age

They want modern wood

With no history

No cracks

No humidity

No air

No piano solos

I have a soul

Only a few can see it

Maybe in ten years

More will see past my reputation.

II
Sky

Part II

SKY

FLASH

The message came to me in aspects of amethyst

and coils of tawny cream. It was a loud

jarring noise that shook the sky

and my nervous system. The blackness

of the clouds did not frighten me

as much as the pit of my stomach did.

I ran home and removed the leash

from my dog to shut the lights. My

phone buzzed and startled me.

My eyes could barely focus

everyone left

and I wondered

What if I never see my family again?

My husband was at work

my kids were on other continents

and the future never looked so

ominous as the bolts

shook the trees

the scattered leaves

the trampled debris

the used coffee cup lids

the broken masks

the rocky dirt

it shook the invisible air

as I stared at my phone

and my soul confides in me

this is why you need

to listen to me

because you never

know when the end

of the world

will occur.

FULL MOON JULY 13, 2022

Feel its white cotton energy

enter your skin

shed the monthly toxins

as you breathe in the new moon

sit under it

walk under it

sing or dance under it

like my daughters and sisters

once did

do it today

keep the moon close

rejuvenate your soul

let the power become your song

let the blueberry darkness

become your peach light

no need for alphabetical rituals

only your divine presence

your gentle existence

under its milky whiteness.

THE CHIRP

The language of birds

is one that has no definition

in this unpigmented realm

it tells a story

in the eventide sky

in the nightfall trees

on a dusk branch

on your front and back porch

on the top of the beanstalk skyscrapers

they keep trying to live with us

scared when we get too close

rightfully so

they have seen how humans treat wildlife

they are the most unique

live a life

we envy

Free as a bird they say

If I could be an animal I would be a bird

they fly from Paris to England

from lengthy lakes to battered buildings

clasping their rare voice

in the solid air

communicating with each other

by song not words

no error for miscommunication

the message is as clear as the full moon

or a rainy day

for many, it is cryptic

lightworkers, healers, star seeds

know that birds chirping

can replace any anti-depressant medication

birds search for worms in the earth

as we try to not step on them on concrete

their chirp can wake you up early

to tweet has taken on a whole new meaning

once upon a time it meant

the chirp of a young baby bird

now it's a social media post.

The deeper we get inside

satellite dishes

Wi-Fi connections

IP addresses

the further from a flock of birds

lined up on a telephone wire

higher than the nearest tree

come up for air

let the devices run out of battery

and

die.

Look up and try to decipher

the words to their song

birds are chirping today

they have a lot to say

Are you listening?

Are you trying to comprehend

the meaning of the lyrics?

Or are you still scrolling?

It is up to you to listen to the honest voice inside you

outside you

and around you.

ATMOSPHERE

Spaceships, satellites, in the exosphere

Exo, outside, outdoors, out there

    Somewhere unsafe yet kind

Aurora surrounds us in the thermosphere

    Cold, colder, coldest, survival for the few

    Who speak an unchartered, undetected language

Meteors, meteorological rockets in the mesosphere

    Meso, inside, indoors, in here

    The place in your soul no one can touch

Radiosonde, radio sound-waves in the stratosphere

    Under pressure, filled with messages

    The second layer of the atmosphere

Singing its songs

    Hot air balloons, passenger planes in the troposphere

    No space or time is constant

    No ozone

        A cloud of poems

           For humans to not fear.

OUTER SPACE

When the plants move and sing

there are no roads

to choose a path for them.

The darkness of time

tastes of copper

They say nothing lasts forever

except it does

in this abyss.

Oh, boy! Does it ever

Oh, girl! Does it surprise your timeline

to not scroll

on this part of the black edge

of nothingness.

When time is an endless

song on loop

why wonder about

the Northern and Southern days

watch as spaceships

find their way in the pitch blackness

of time

without numbers.

SUN

I cut yellow construction paper

into thin rectangular lines

slightly uneven

natural rays

       des rayons de soleil

I tell the children to cut inside

       the black circle

       around the circle *le soleil*

I guide the young hands to glue

       the rectangles around the circle

       on fait le soleil

I give them oil pastels

       to draw the face of lights

       un soleil qui brille

Each art a little masterpiece

as if children already know

that every time you look at the sun

it appears different.

MOON

Every month you look at us poets

    and wink

        I'm back, you say

Every month you have a new name

    and grin

        Be creative, you whisper

Every month you choose a number

    and calculate

        Look at the signs, you demand

Every month you show your true self

    and wait

        Do you believe me now, you sing

Every month you never disappoint

and laugh

> *How much more proof do you need,* you ask

Every month you light up the sky

    and write a new book

        Read me, you write.

PLANETS

Do not give up on your fight

Time and space have no concept of why

Pull up your blinds and let in the golden light.

All together you shine bright.

In the darkness where nothing can lie

Do not give up on your fight

Astronomers analyze your width and height

Without sleep, without food, all they did was try

Pull up your blinds and let in the golden light

Greek gods and goddesses examined you in close sight

Epic myths leaving one with a deep sight

Do not give up on your fight.

Once you were nine, now you are eight

Poets writing you poems of a desperate goodbye

Pull up your blinds and let in the golden light.

Oh, Mercury, Venus, Earth, your heart turns love to hate

Oh, Mars, Jupiter, Saturn, Uranus, Neptune, your darkness is a high

Do not give up on your fight

Pull up your blinds and let in the golden light.

STARS

You have human flesh

your background is black

golden sparkles on your shirts

in a field of Matcha green tea

      orange passion fruit

           yellow apples

                forgotten winter leaves

you both stand

one taller than the other

you may have been in my womb

once, but that was in another life

you can bend space

and make it sparkle

from the inside out.

You are my screen saver

a photo I took under gray skies

two of you, as one being

yet not the same

that is the magic about stars

no one knows

exactly where they come from

only that they are.

CONSTELLATIONS

Before clocks and maps

before punching cards and gaps

before you ever met me

Capricorn and Aquarius

had a philosophical discussion about

soul mates

Pisces and Aries

cried over old romance movies

Taurus and Gemini

argued about the best and the worst

of everything

Cancer and Leo went to the theater

for different reasons

Virgo and Libra were twin flames

Scorpio and Sagittarius went on an adventure

of the soul

and Ophiuchus was a lone wolf.

DAYTIME SKY

Hi, I'm Orion.
Can you see me?

Only when I close my eyes

I'm hundreds of light years away
Yet I'm free as if I'm next to you

Hey there, I'm Ainilam.
I'm the farthest star
From Earth. I like my stillness.
Humans are jealous of my privacy.

When I close my eyes
I see nothing.

We did not invent you.

All the countries invented you

gave you different names.

But we all know

That you hide your true movement

But since the first tree sprouted

Your myths and legends

Gave us roots and stories.

I see you at night too.

NIGHT SKY

The way a masquerade party

invites secrecy

the way bombs jolt you to a new trauma

it is a proclamation of surprise

intense readings you cannot decipher

try as you may

your eyes move upwards

as you take your dog for his last walk

of the night.

It is past dinnertime

tea time, Ovaltine time

dessert time, bedtime

every night when you look up

the moon is telling you *today*

or

not today.

The way you were led astray

by men you try to forget

the way you drank so many shots

and kissed the wrong man

it is a proclamation of your soul

a wireless telegraph between

    you

    and

    the

    night.

CLOUDS

Perhaps you want to tell me

a story every day

in your own artistic language

or maybe you like to

play childish games of wonder

to adults who think they

have outgrown you

I do not need to know how quintessential

you are in the atmosphere

or how you pass your days

Imagine the billions of poems

dedicated to your presence

How many dead fathers and mothers

traveled through your gates

to find the light

Perhaps you like your secrets

to remain unsaid

that is why your language

can only be heard by

      light beings

Still so many are trying to reach you

      by lifting their arms

           will you bend down and rain on all of us?

your refraction on the window

recalls a time of skipping with friends

and shouting, "Look, look, a rainbow."

SMOG

He wears a mask to breathe/ his job is outdoors/ visiting temples and parks/ forbidden cities / explaining / telling the same story every week / he says / it's seventy-five percent pollution today / we take pictures and videos / as tourists ofen do.

POLLUTION

In China I saw the smog

                      on the tip of my love

put flowers behind my ears

                      I was pushed around

for

being too sensitive

                      A robot brought us

our toilet paper

humans and robots the same soul

                      drones kept tabs on

                      our walks

our tour guide wore a mask before covid ever existed

                      I saw how much pain

earth was in

I felt that something strong and fierce will break us soon

                                                      we beat her up, she
fights back

it is a natural disaster

                                                      I had to travel so far

to see what is in front of me.

KITES

I sit down to write my novel in a Parisian cafe

I see it.

It is blue, orange, red, yellow, purple

all the colors of the chakra

look down at me

a pilgrimage to my soul

as eyes are on me. I know

those eyes. My soul has a memory.

No romantic gestures, no playlists,

no lyrics, no serenades, no violin.

Eyes and kites are silent

they move in motion to air.

The air you inhabit is mine

as we both look up

at the sky and you say *You look familiar*

    So do you

we look back up but the kite

falls down on a young boy

who pulls its strings.

That is the story of how we first met in 1939

Ocean

PART III

OCEAN

THE SEA ALSO RISES

I am aware that every year I age
like the children and grandchildren
and great grandchildren I have
held in my arms.
We have seen first births
last and final breaths
we have celebrated birthdays
retirements, unwanted deaths
going away barbecue parties
welcoming ones.

I age as much as you do
but oh, so differently
the wind makes my walls weak
the sea turns them into creaks
into ancient erosion
the high waters flood my concrete bricks

the waves sink my memories

you have of me

I make you feel a certain way

I have held your tears

on the pillow, on the bed, on my floor

that creaks with ghosts who speak to me

come back day after day.

I am grateful you clean me

and collect all my dust balls

I breathe easier when you open

my windows

let the air in

you have sat in front of my shutters

contemplating life, wondering about

your future, regretting your past

your human thoughts seep through the furniture

the buffet your great grandma bought

when she built the house.

By 2050, once your son has his daughter
I will no longer exist.

Take a photo of what we leave of our family
in front of the house, with a view of the Sea.

It keeps rising. I see it every day.
I mark it as you did in the children's closet
with a sharpened pencil
and the height of each child
my destruction is not yours yet
but it is a step closer
to your death.

Come visit me as if it is your last
Come sleep as if you have no other bed.

When I rise, you fall.

When I no longer exist, you will mourn
      for all the things you
         never sold at the estate sale
      that never happened.

Money has no value in the sea
      under the water
      it floats and rises
like dead fish.

WAVES

I cannot replicate the movement

nature has a way of healing wounds

no amount of discussions can do

it is in the way his skin tingles

as hers bounces to the foam

you would think that at forty-nine

he would outgrow his broken heart

but she only makes it matter more

at all he has been trying so hard to forget.

SHORE

Even a photo does not do it justice

stop being stuck in one spot

move to the seashell filled shore

where you will finally fill up your storage

with sand on your toes

and love in your bones.

Give the phone away

to an android who needs it

when you require fake lives less and less

the startled shore becomes clear

truth is not a manic illusion

be careful who you call a rational guru

do not fall for the wrong lines

repetitive words

in different mouths

kisses can be traps in memories

promises can be hooks on a fishing line

once you get caught

the shore will only be in the far distant

but once you unpack

smelling the salt water

you will finally be home.

IONIAN

She flows out from the Mediterranean Sea

Her separation includes

    Calabria, Sicily, Albania,

        Greece.

Did you see any olive groves

    spinster cypresses

        willful wildflowers

            pearly pebbles

If you cannot see them

        you can feel them close by

It is warmer because she is a sensual one

Her attributes lie under her skin

        when you feel her

She knows how to open your silence up

how to let her inner wisdom heal

The sight of her makes you gasp

      for   her   air

It seems her legs have no chapter endings

              no novel beginnings

a reflection of her crying soul.

    You never say *enough now*

only *I want more.*

AEGEAN

My history is ancient and involves this
       monumental place
where my civilization flourished

It holds all the battles in its waves
       stones of warriors defeating
and still all I can think about
when I look out from it

is the future of us
and how one day in a new lifetime

we will sit in front of it
and it will be ours for a while
our souls will come together
after fifty years of living apart.

RIVER

You live between two cities
follow different lives

one would say
you have a double life

like a married man having an affair
you seem to move through the earth

without thought, yet your flow
can sometimes run dry

dissolve into canyons and valleys
in places lovers meet in secrecy

you take your stories
and guard them in your vault

but when you overflow with emotions

our cities flood from your tears

we think you cannot see us or hear our cries

but you are the first to notice

our sadness floating like plastic straws.

LAKE

You hold us temporarily
in your arms. You are so
still at times. You barely
seem to breathe.
You know how to keep
us cool and how to
let us go.
You are the best parent
to children.

They love you
unconditionally.

You hold so many wishes

in pennies

unspoken

imagine all the secrets drowned

in your presence

You would have been a famous author

but your silence is your secret

Your silence keeps us coming back

in an endless cycle of time.

SHELLS

A seal life lived inside me once

I protected it

now you find me washed up

on the beach you booked your trip on

young kids make me dizzy

with the amount of time they wash

and play with me

I enjoy their company

they know how to be in the moment with me

It is the sad poets who put me in a bag

take me back to their house

Take me out of the plastic bag that has killed my soul

place me in a jar

people love to stare at me

sometimes pick me up

some are sadder than others

the jar locks me inside out

I dream of the beach

and the kids building sandcastles around me

I miss my home

they do not understand I need the sand

a colorful ashtray is not in my future

      or a painted bowl

      or a pearl earring

I would rather be a child's art

than an adult's dead dream.

PEBBLES

Colorful shapes and shades

smooth as satin and rough as sandpaper

from cotton white to somber gray

I hold one in my hand

> *you cannot find your future in the past*

I pick up another one

> *please don't take me away from my friends*
>
> *we've been together for centuries*

I put one in my pocket

> *I want to be alone. I need more silence.*

I feel them under my toes.

> *This is where I must be. Holding up your energy.*

I bend to pick up a burgundy one.

I've been waiting for you my whole life.

PACIFIC

Ferdinand Magellan

sailed in 1519 to discover

pacificus tranquil ocean

if he only knew in 2022

how a young boy found

empty water bottles

    broken cell phones

        old desk chairs

            used tires

at the Great Pacific Garbage Patch

and understood a new tragedy of life.

The Ring of Fire

holds the grace of the coral reef

three quarters of the world's volcanoes

this ocean shrinks one inch every year

whales and seals searching for food

sea lions and sea turtles

stuck in a man-made tourist trap

under the water

Mother Earth reacts

effects of the plate tectonics

the plastic in an animal's mouth

in 1519, Magellan

never thought this tranquility

would become a destruction.

SEA OF ATLAS

Screaming sea lion

recurring oil spills

    never-ending pollution

marvelous manatees

    one fifth of Gaia's breath

green, brown, yellow, black sea turtles

    accidental nets fishing breaking time

gregarious gravel

    stunning stones brought to your home

in your pathway, walkway, bathroom, kitchen

    toxic substance dumps

diaphanous dolphins dancing delightfully

    oil spills choking the unseen

growing one inch every year

    Greek mythological creatures creeping up

wonderful whales washing the waves

    running rivers ravaged inside

saltiest of them all

      gargle and giggle geometrical gems

mud masks and algae

      anti-aging and cancer

admire an astounding albatross

      burdened with life and death

kissing you from a distance

      on a land you no longer visit.

WATER

She is in my herbal tea
      the morning black coffee
colorful water bottles children drink from
      the splashing of my face
           to eliminate the night.

She is in my detox soup
      homemade vegetable stock
garden vegetables
      lavender plant
plants are thirsty for her
      without her they die
      droughts
      hunger
      pain
      loss of life

She is in my lemon water

      peppermint

      strawberry

      mint blend

her talent lies in existing.

She is in my body

she broke her womb inside me

for my children to arrive

I broke out of her to breathe air.

BLUE

Look up or down in the middle of the ocean
> *Blue*

I see you everywhere I go *Skye blue*

I wear them every day. *Denim*

She gave you a bracelet to protect you
> *Lapis Lazuli*

The children wear their uniform to school
> *Navy blue*

My Virgo birthstone has its power over you
> *Sapphire*

The evil eye protects you *Persian blue*

I kept one of his onesies to never forget
> *Baby blue*

The way his eyes stare at me in a rage *Steel blue*

The couch we made love on in the middle of a war
    Vivid Cerulean

The place we would meet in our next lifetime
    Egyptian blue

Our tears when we said our last goodbye
    Indian blue

The first time we met in Montreal *Blue green.*

SPLASH

I am the splash in your water

I am the bounce in your footsteps

I am the keys to your piano.

I am water. You are water.

When we kiss, we are splashing.

You are the splash in my bath

You are the wind in my day

You are the voice in my mind.

You are water. I am water.

When we met, we splashed lifetimes.

They are the cliffs in our path They
are the rocks under our feet They
are the shores of our past. When
we parted, we started.

ANIMALS IN THE OCEAN

Did you not see the movement?

      Do not jump

they will not bite

      leave them swim

as you are.

A jellyfish bit Maria once in Cuba

      John pissed on it

a shark bit a child in Cape Cod

marine biologists kissed sea lions in private.

There is no blessing in being so unaware.

I want to know the name of each animal

but what is the point

they do not want to know our names.

      We are all unique, like them

and labeling them animals

and us humans

does not make us human at all

we are all animals in the ocean

and no one needs to know our names at all.

DOCK

Your wood holds old lovers

new lovers

lost lives

it holds up memories like statues

You are static in a wild background

grounding us from destruction

with your universal silence

When my husband and I first sat together

in the middle of the night

in 1985

we knew

all the secrets you kept

to yourself.

IV

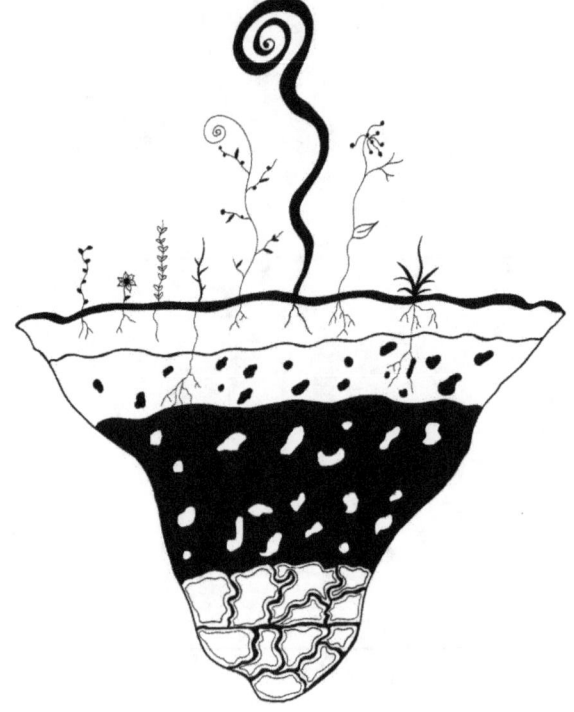

Soil

PART IV

SOIL

earth

I dig with my hands

to find your roots

but you are everywhere.

When I was a child

I pulled worms out of you

and when I showed an adult your beauty

they yelled at me,

"Don't touch that!"

I found you so fascinating

smooth yet bumpy

I wished for a second

I was you.

dirt

You were on my elbows

knees, clothes, and shoes

my grandma washed you off me

and my stained clothes

I kept finding you

I could not escape your arms

I learned how to jump on you

hug you

put you in my pocket

spit you out

but most of all

I learned how to cherish you

when no adult did.

solids

No matter how much force is used

                            against you

you are a fierce resistance of enemies

if he applies his love bombing

                            you apply your armor

your molecules are packed together

                            like a family living in one bedroom

no hate can pull you apart.

This rigidity of yours is envious

of all the other three

states of matter

the other would never tell you

just like a husband and wife have secrets

they take it to the grave—

with the least amount of kinetic energy.

liquids

You work well under pressure

with your definite, constant volume

chasing away a fixed shape

you are free to flow

in a cup of warm herbal tea

Greek honey

A tall glass of lemon water

in every vein of a human body

    we cannot live with or without you

    on a flight

    in a prison

    on a campground

    at a dinner party

    squeezed out of a fresh orange

cheering with you at a wedding

placing you in a diffuser

    to filtrate the air with spring

filling up my car to drive

eating you in a cup of cinnamon for dessert

becoming sober and saying no to your toxins

drinking you green

and saying yes to your antidote

        cure

        elixir.

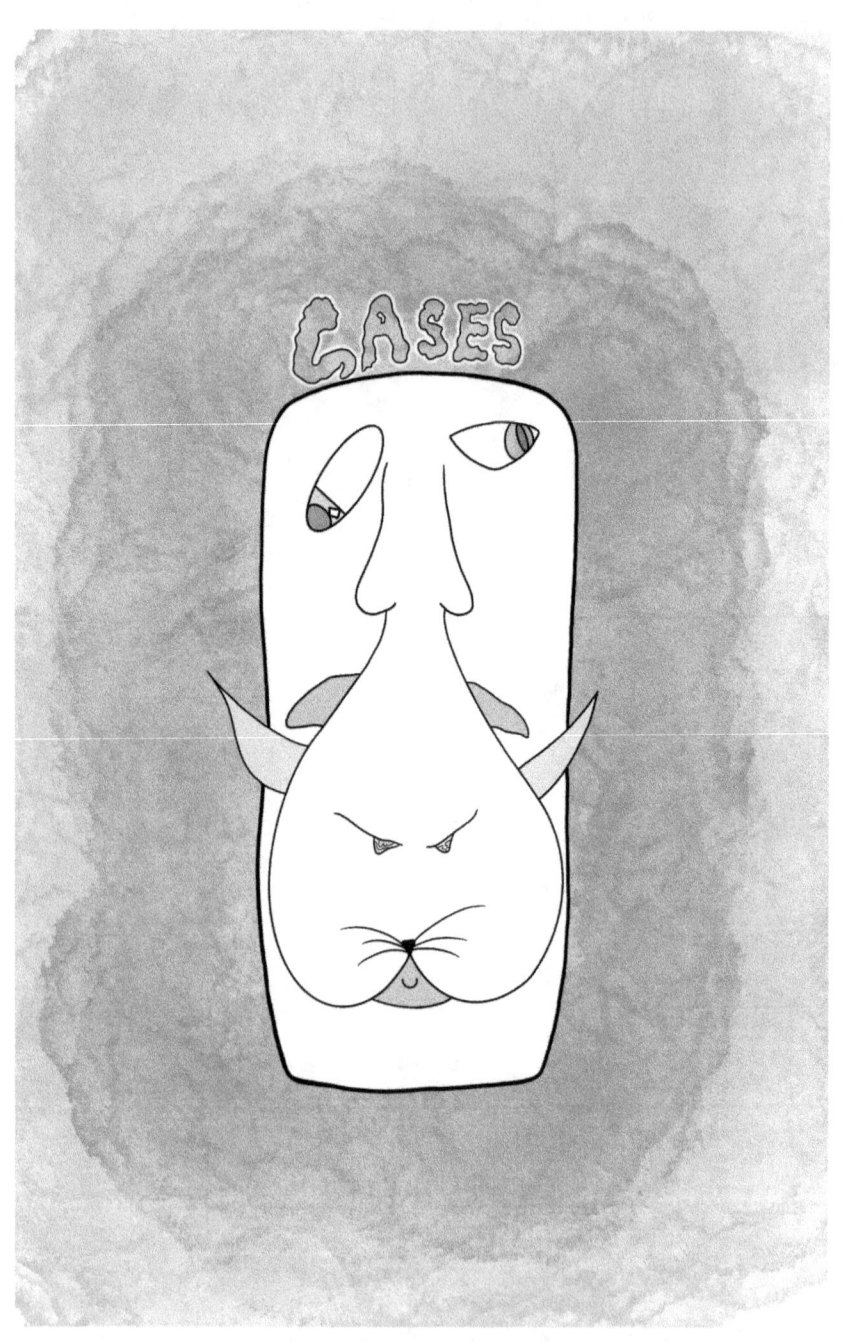

gases

I could not breathe without you
you hand me my oxygen like a gift

too much of you can kill me
you are shapeless, formless

a chameleon among matter.

Hot air balloons will not survive without you
our earth needs your protective blanket

you are required to make fertilizers for food
nylon for stockings, shirts, pants,
dyes for fabric
explosives for war.

Without you, cars stall

smells disintegrate

you can be toxic

pure

elemental

mixed

in ways no one else can

in moments of joy and terror,

you take the shape of everything

wherever you go

like a vagabond among men.

minerals

I could make you a list
      an old-fashioned recipe book of traditional meals
I could plant you a garden
         bake you a cake with the right cup of love
connect to your playlist
         and geometrical shapes
yet I know the essentials
      drop notes, poems, messages in my ear every day
they grieve my books so I no longer look for a muse

foods say
      listen to your own voice first

I could write another erotic book
I could text you all my thoughts
invite you over for dopamine benefits
with time, space, love

minerals turn into

colorful crystals

like the brown and purple one I gave you

I never told you

one was me, the other you

keep them together so that one day

we will be side by side and touch again

to function normally

feeding off our energy.

organisms

Five kingdoms on earth

a tree of life

in the places you did not look

fungus to kill you gently with ease

unaware of bacteria tearing your sadness

up into tiny pieces of unwritten poems

Oh, those dead animals you called the city about

the dead raccoon on the service road

between Dagenais and highway 440

it was laying there for days

Let the lavender plant bring peace into a home

place it near a window

with lots of sun

and right on the surface of your tomato garden

you see protists

those direct food sources

those decomposed

that can give and destroy

live on soil

in water

be sexual / asexual

a parasite

hard to conquer

hard to love.

organic matter

Colorful leaves falling down from maple trees

cut grass in the compost

clipped flower stems at the end of October

broken branches in schoolyards for children to play with and throw

moss in my flowerbed at dawn

algae in shades of unseen brown

lichens crawling on my salty skin

marine feeding the soil and vegetable sewage sludge

sawdust from the newly renovated home

insects living in the walls

earthworms on the grass

on the one-way street

in the pounding earth

microbes causing cancer

covid

viruses

fungi

leGng bacteria ring your doorbell

all the dead plants

coming back to life

through soil.

V

Tea

PART V

TEA LEAVES

TEA LEAVES

Reused glass jars full of love
        I take my Sharpie, masking tape
        label each one
        different sizes, different purposes
chamomile
        sage
        Greek mountain tea
        herbal mix of Cretan flowers
        mint
add them all in my stone tea kettle
open up my recipe book with my remedies

Sabrina told me
        in all my past lives I was a witch
        they burned my herbal remedies book
        they hung me
        I keep coming back

      to write more books

      to watch them burn

I planted my herbs this summer

      I placed each one in a new journal

      named them

 put my hand underground

I made tea leaves to continue all my lives in this one

      it feels as if I know what to do

      how to cut the cinnamon bark

      how much ginger to add

      understand that basilisk flowers need to be dried

      to help with digestion

I know so much without reading one book

      all my lives are here now

      take out the Royal Albert Fine Bone China

      from another generation

      pour the tea

      heal anyone who rings my bell.

I met a man at a book fair in Toronto

he said your name means "God, Christ and witch in Italian

Christ and *Striga* the perfect balance."

I know what to think now.

My reality has shifted.

GREEN TEA

You are light on your feet

      but you are strong as a tiger

a distinct taste

      for those who know your curing benefits

the mildness of your taste

      the timid aroma is like a tree in your background

please do not cut it because it has too many leaves
I am not a prophet, but they need you more than you think

instead of a cigarette, drink a cup

      to revive your incarnation

you make my mind stop tossing and turning
somehow, I am calm when you are on my lips

and travel inside so close

to my crying heart

drinking you is healing my spirit

and making room for more love.

SAGE

I planted you in my garden this summer

    when you sprouted

        my heart leaped as if I saw my lover out of place

I dried you up, removed your stem oh so gently

    put you in a jar

    in my pot

    in my life

    drank you, burned you,

    smudged you,

    spoke to your smoke

I read once I could add you to tomato sauce

    meat dishes

eggs

soups

broths

fish

    and

now I love you even more

    for all the ways

you recreate yourself.

COLOR

When her stomach hurts
  she blames her heart for being in love
  with the wrong man
she only eats organic food
  no tea bags
    she researched the chemicals

he got married to the woman who does not see him

she thinks if she pours him a cup first,
  he will love her more
she wrote a poem and left the kettle on
  he had almost finished his cup
she found it odd when she poured her tea
her cup was full
she split in two
never thinking for once

      he took his without thinking of her

he was on the phone

      did not realize

she had a broken heart

      and it was only 10:08 in the morning

with a yellow cup of tea

because she put too much turmeric

It is not something to argue about

how can she prove she thinks of others *first*

she doubts her own self

and how many cups of water she poured

she never accepts the facts

she doubts them

to keep giving

even when there's nothing left to give

she talks walks

to never forget how easily her heart breaks

over the color of the tea.

YOUR FUTURE

They say your future is in the tea leaves

but all I see is the past

shame on me

for letting the men do what they did

Even if it almost happened

shame on me for not predicting

my future. How could I know

I would marry my absent father?

My great-grandfather's betrayal

lurks inside my veins. How could

I know I could never

replace my father? How could

I know no one / no man /

Could love me the same?

I had him for thirty-nine years
did not realize how

precious that time was

I kept looking at my future

trying to be a good girl

a dutiful daughter

a perfect wife

and other such nonsense

when all I did was bad shit

to make the future

so full of heartache

I'd write books about other nonsense

to avoid my true self

they say your future is in the tea leaves
but I am Greek

we read the coffee cups
the symbols transform into words

this poem is about all the Mothers on Earth
who try to predict the future

and keep repeating their past

this poem plants seeds in wounds

untouched by human eyes

some traumas are too difficult to speak

to Write, to Burn.

CLOVES

I kept the twenty-year-old spice shaker

they do not make them the same way

the whales are smaller now

there were some cloves left

when romance dies

what do you do with her spice jar?

You pass it on

to the next generation

like jewelry

and now I add it to my iron cast kettle

when I drink a cup

my mother-in-law is inside of me too

a piece of the universe

closed off from the world

waiting to be handled gently

like a young child.

CINNAMON BARK

Planted in Sri Lanka

and all I could think about

are young children

on a farm

cutting them up

into little pieces

to package

for the grocery store

with hungry stomachs

and discipline.

CHAMOMILE

Yellow flowers

Pleasant dreams

Your sun-like appearance

Taught ancient Egyptians

To offer you to the Sun god

You were used

For incense

And now most people

Need you before bed

So many anxiety disorders

These rabbit days

So many snickering chemicals

But none as pure as you

You are as soft as cotton

Subtle as a Spanish guitar melody

Coy as a cat under your balcony

Proud as a mother

Your comfort makes you vulnerable

Honest as a child

Cheerful as a Mardi Gras parade

No one can change you

That is your devoted superpower

You can shine golden

Attracting cures.

VERVAIN

Anxious people love you

For being there for them

Reliable, you.

You can recite all

The lives you have saved

You can tell us

How suicide

Is your enemy

You can hear the voices

Others cannot

Your talent

    Lies in all

    The hidden languages

    Buried in a past

Reinvented.

CRETAN HERBS

I made you more humane than I should have. Gave you all these attributes to create an image I no longer see. It all stems from the root, the colors, and the fragrance. I tried to pack you into a jar so tightly, but you overflowed with heartache. I know I made you up. Plath said it best. No poet comes close to her writing. I wanted you to be someone else. I'm sorry. You're no longer able to simmer for me. You burned me with your heat.

TURMERIC

In my ginger red lentil soup

you grow stronger

I add some black pepper

and you become a Superpower

In a chewable tablet I swallow you

the taste is divine

I have no more aches

My entire body is feeling fine.

In my tea I sprinkle you

Or chop you up

my fingers turn yellow like the sun

you have a party in my stomach, oh what fun

Your color makes me smile

Lights up candles, create lattes

while all the while

you sit quietly on my shelf in complete denial

to your flame throwing abilities.

VI
Coffee beans

Part VI

COFFEE BEANS

BLEND

In the ground, I am alone
next to my family

when I am combined with you
we create a delicious cup

of two different coffee beans
distinct taste

I could be part Persian, Greek
you could be part Italian, Scottish

together we make a perfect sip.

WHOLE

Learning to live alone on earth

is how art creates itself

I was born this way

my being is part oval

part round

a peculiar shape

you buy me at a grocery store

but did you know

I have tears

and cry when you crush me?

and swim when you drink me?

ESPRESSO

I found my espresso machine

filled it with kisses

organ music

understood its loneliness

after all these years

to be refilled with fresh water

and let the first snowfall

be silent.

GOLD-LEAF ROYAL ALBERT

Perhaps you were meant for afternoon tea

quiet Sunday mornings

less cageful spite

workings of your inner child

perhaps the nights are too long

but you have no choice but

to sit pretty

in your teal, black, yellow, blue, colors

leaf handles

delicate surprise

I poured cinnamon inside your hand

while you hold my hope

in a few sweltering slurps.

GIVING YOU UP

I thought I would want you

every morning

upon the opening of my eyes

and my first yoga stretches.

I thought you would keep me company

at my desk

while I wrote my future sixth novel.

I thought your grains

filled me with innovative ideas

I read once you saturated with

the seeds to sprout truth

I ached for you

had sharp pains of neglect from you

In the evening, I had my full

but once I woke up

you filled my veins with a desire

You gave me power to spread my branches

connect to the falling first snowfall

in November

I have tried to stop this need

yet keep coming back to you

for more of what you can offer me

like a lover going back to a moment never forgotten

I drink every ounce of you

yet know

I am giving you up tomorrow

I am giving up the addiction

the nervous love you offer me

this kind of love must be called something else

it takes away my capacity

to be roots in a tree

it twists my reality

into long winding paths

of self-defense

it makes my voice change colors

melts upon hitting the cold earth

I have known for decades I need to give you up

but my ego was not ready

until now.

GRAINS

Honesty comes in spurts of doubt

along the coast of Brazil

In the 18th century the discovery of it

was not the sight of the first rainbow

before that no one can say

how plants brewed a black drink.

Lies sprout from human greed

to create a colorful illusion

of collected stamps from New Guinea

coffee from South American organic farms

a swipe or a scroll or a like or a share

for the projected fame

not the behind the scene unwashed cups.

COFFEEHOUSE

Cappuccino with almond milk, no sugar

espresso

cafe latte with oat milk, one sugar

all day she takes the orders

creates zigzags, leaves, hearts, designs, letters

as her tip jar piles high like snow on a mountain

she is so proud of her work

gives it to you as if it were a painting at a museum

she is somewhat of a healer

her precise stop and go as her hands flow like water

tell you passionate love stories

her imagination soars and intensifies at her peak hour

you should know

she hates public speaking

yet she brings prosperity

with every sip you say *great coffee*

we all send her positive vibes and social media stories

she smiles once in a while in photos

you forget her name

most of the time she is caught in action

and you see how much she loves

to make the best coffee

it is in her body movement

not her words, or her tip jar

that humble gratitude

awareness

of doing what you love

without judgment or care

justified by the aroma

of casual

categorical coffee.

INSTANT

All this immediate gratification
in a cup of love

you take moments away
from the future

in a decision
that needs the slowness of a turtle

Some thoughts are best left unsaid
words cannot be swallowed for long

eventually they regurgitate
melt inside the sugar and cream

snap your fingers
still, you don't have the glass jar

ready to be reused with spices

and a new label.

ORGANIC

If the instant you wake up
you think *coffee!*

you are addicted to these words
and the way they make you stand up

sit down, analyze
when you break up with someone

you never forget the way
they loved you

no matter how bad it was
even bad love is unforgettable

the mold does not live only in walls
it is in your gut

in your dark coffee blend

read the labels

save yourself

from food

who ever thought

a cup of coffee could kill you?

OUR FIRST MEETING

You ordered espresso

I had a latte

the red and white tablecloths

stuck to your elbow

you said I had mysterious eyes

I watched your mouth

as you spoke. No tarot card

reading prepared me for

the first taste of coffee

with you.

Nothing tastes like your language

your silence, your words

the most drinkable sentence

the moment replays in my mind

with no credit rolls.

Herbs

VII

Part VII

HERBS

CORIANDER

Adding you to my arugula salad

Turmeric soup with ginger

Guacamole dip

Your richness fights

The soreness in my bones

You make my heart pound

With African drum beats

From another distant life.

My blood sugar owes you

All its sweetness

You reduced my salt intake

Your natural compounds

Boost me with eternal life.

MINT

Thank you for all the ways

you enter me

revive my senses

I remember my lovers

because of you

I remember my dead relatives

talk to their spirit

my cold symptoms disappear

when I breathe you into my air flow.

Thank you for all the ways

you enter me

when I chew your tiny leaves

or drink you in a warm cup of tea

all my ailments turn into flowers

It is accessible to add you

to my pasta sauce

        egg salad

        sweet desserts

delicious smoothies

but most of all

when I see your leaves

floating in my glass of water

it brings me

daily gifts from the universe.

DILL

Peas, carrots, potatoes, onion, dill
                tomato sauce

lettuce, shallots, cucumber, dill
feta cheese, olive oil, vinegar, then toss

Greek yogurt, cucumber, garlic
dill, olive oil, blend

spinach, dill, leeks, parsley, olive oil
feta, egg, new trend.

LAVENDER

I have many voices to bring you out of the sun. I have a voice to soothe your childhood trauma when your father beat up your dreams with a tree branch. I have another tone to my voice that is high with fear, fear of snakes, fear of the sea, of the dark, and fear of the night demons. You planted me in a pot in May. By the time July came around, my emotional baggage sprouted. I had to feel your calm nature, your children's voices, and musical instruments playing under the sun next to me on your deck. All these headaches, bug bites, and inflammation I had miraculously healed you. My voice is powerful. It can make your midnight sweats take a pause; it listens to the words your hair speaks and lets them write poetry. Your hair had a feather pen, and it wrote stanzas on moods, stress, and anxiety. Who needs medication when you have me so close? Use me on your skin, your face, and your heart. Drop my oil in your steaming bath. Drink me in your tea. I am grateful to you for hearing my voice. Spread the word in tiny circles. I do not need social media. I need you to keep talking to me to hear my voice from 2500 years ago.

ROSEMARY

Your leaves are further apart

Sturdy like a stop sign

Thin yet full of iron

Your vitamins fuel me

Like gas in a car

There I am

At a bar

Drinking a glass of water

Asking for a sprig of rosemary.

The bartender is in a sour mood

Looks confused

Anxious about his tip

Hates that I do not conform

I wait for his answer

"No" he replies coldly.

"Well, it benefits heart health." I reply.

He wears glasses
And pushes them higher.

I don't wait for a reply

I think of the plant
In front of Mom's back porch
How she cuts it
And dries it
And grinds it
Puts it in a used spice jar with love
And writes
    ROSE MARY in her handwriting
I hold on to it
Until the day
I need to read it over and over again.

ITALIAN BASILISC

She floats in my glass

Never sinks

I watch as her medicinal healing

Adds its remedy to my h20

She smells like pasta sauce

Tastes like a light morning chill

She spoke to me during my darkest days

Of loneliness

Told me her secrets

To happiness

She said to keep looking at her height

Her top, her bottom

Listen to her piano solos

Her fingers tell endless

Stories of curing the soul

From inked blotches.

She stayed up late with me

Watching me think of words

To write to ex-lovers

Who are happier without me

She makes my house smell of cursive writing

Her attitude is fierce as a battered woman

Escaping her life

In the summer, she sits in her comfortable

Quebec soil

In the winter, she is next to my kitchen sink

Under Santorini rocks

Ready to be trimmed

And live her second life

She has no past lives

She lives once

And recalls only the moment

She floats

And gives her being up

To support yours, mine, theirs,

Ours.

Her life is now

We can learn so much

From one basil plant

We ignore in the supermarket

For 3.99.

Grazie por l'amore.

GREEK BASIL

1.

In 326 A.D Empress Helene

bent down to see what shone on the grass

her fingers tingled

her body shivered

it was a cross

gold or brass

she could not tell

it was in her hands now

glowing

when she looked down at the spot

she noticed an herb was growing

on the earth

in the shape of a cross,

her hand smelled sweet

the aroma awakened

her senses

I will name this herb

Vasilik

Basil

of the Kind

she walked with the cross on the country road

joy in her heart

gratitude in her soul

a sick woman stopped the Empress

Can I kiss the cross? She asked.

Yes, the Empress handed her the cross

a day later, the sick woman

turned healthy

and the Empress Helene

knew when she bent down

that day

it was God's sign

for her

to believe

and it was said

that Empress Helene

knew it was Jesus's cross

and when you walk into any

Greek household

and look at the back porch

you'll see a pot of Greek basil

kissed by the sun.

2.

She is in my world

because she has no words

to fight you with

no song

to take away from you

no music

to create

only a scent

of a man

who exists in each one of us.

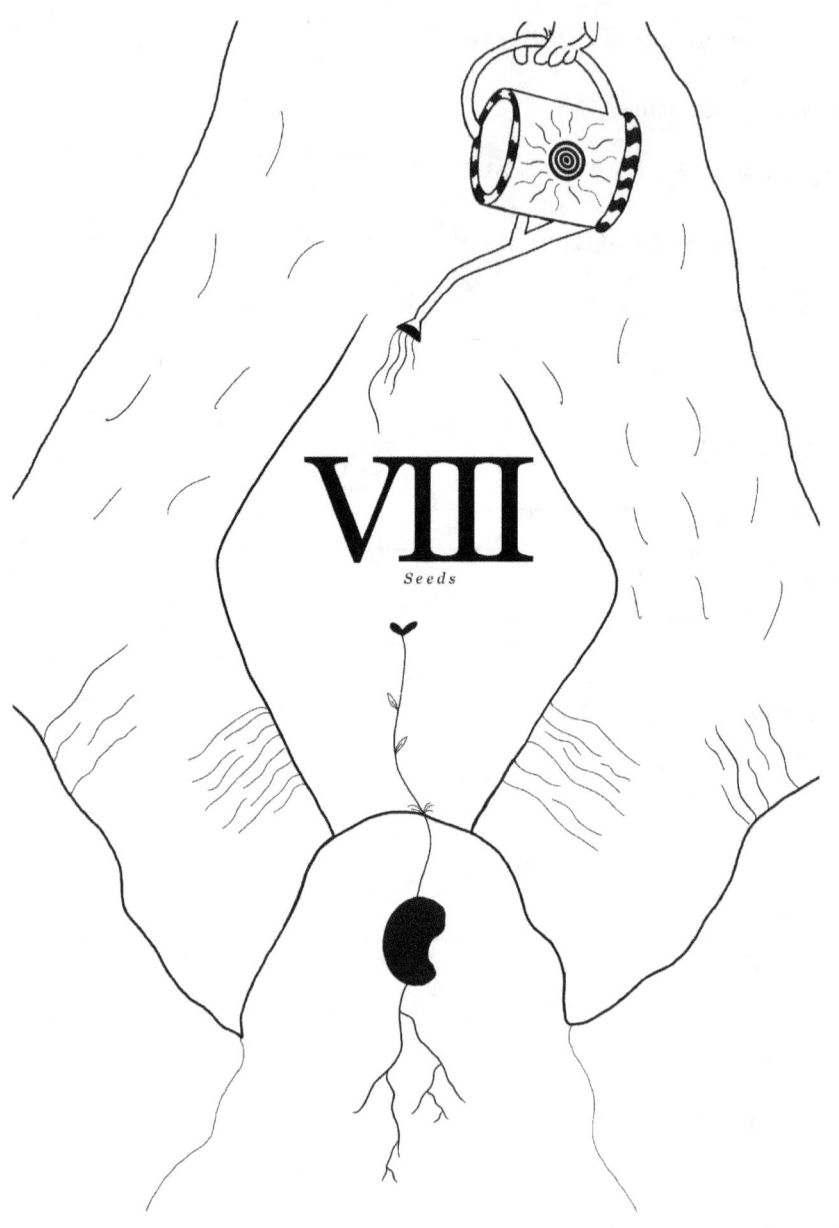

VIII
Seeds

PART VIII

SEEDS

CHOKE

I knew to not swallow you

and yet I did

I knew to not bite into you

and so, I did

life lessons are not spoken

they are experienced

No one says

        You will choke on it

You cannot predict if an apple tree will grow

the right height

just because you planted it

just because you planned it

I knew to not taste you

and yet I did

I knew to not savor you

decades later, I almost died

In the back of my throat

you scratch me with words left unsaid

I knew to not love you

and yet I did.

PLANT

This morning the snow
brought me depth

Spunky jumped in it
until he soaked with time

the kind of time
that blends together as one moment

while years evaporate
no matter how many times you

try to memorize dates.

The water absorbs time
watches it go by

as all your decisions

crash into one pot

one seed

you forgot to water

because you met a girl

or a boy

who you thought

understood the language of seeds

but they pretend to speak it

for you

only you did not

speak it.

You thought you did

you doubted yourself

and all your hair
started to fall out

all your bangs grew
out of your armpits

and reality
shifted once again.

PETAL

I can be creamy white

with dazzling tones of yellow

or as bright as a rainbow

a Mediterranean sunset

overlooking the Aegean Sea.

My scent attracts you

you dream about my horizon

your windowpane

is full of my love

but no matter how many times

you change my water

I will inevitably die of thirst.

You decide to pull me apart

before my time

I have tears, but cannot see them

your dimension hides them

turns them into murky colors,

around my skin

I rest next to my cousins

we are red, purple, yellow

pink petals on a tray

lack of self-worth

brings you our dryness,

months later

I am placed in a dish bowl

your mother-in-law gave you

and you add a dried leaf

who was my sworn enemy

I slump half-dead

yet still breathing the air

as it turns me

into an old wilted lady

within months

you pick me up

and stick me on a bookmark

glue on your fingers

trapping my heart

locked with your words

you brought me back

to my ancestors

preserved on paper

for someone to place

me in a book

where I will finally perish

in peace.

STEM

When she enters the room,

he sees her before everyone does

because the body she was born into

is the one he can never forget

being inside of. He knows it is

more than a root of a flower

he understands how seeds need

soul, water, and sun. Yet on this

day, Nov. 14, 2014, he sees

her sitting on a couch, waiting for him.

She knows what he is supposed

to look like, but knows there is

more to his looks than eyes

and a mouth she dreams

of sucking on

particularly

his lower lip.

He walks over casually

all business like as if meeting her

was a tick on his agenda.

His poker face is transparent to her

she knows he will forget

the past, future, present as she has done.

They are standing now

their hair as petals

their feet as the land

the sun on their skin

the water in their body

as they say

    Hi, nice to meet you

    at the same time

at quarter to seven.

LEAVES

No one wants me
        I serve a better purpose on paper
as a five-year-old draws me as an afterthought

Everyone knows I am part of a greater good
        like a bass player in a rock band
        like the embryo that could not survive
        the first trimester

I like it here. I am content under the sky
in the matrix pretty background
or the color you select to draw me in

To be original
        we all know how boring green is
        and what a shade of jealousy
        it erupts in ex-lovers who will not get over

shimmering skin in hotel rooms.

I am the one you discard

the other woman

the abandoned friend

yet I exist in oxygen

last the longest

I do not abide by a love language

or a lament

I thrive on seasonal loneliness.

FLOWERS

Surrounding me are dead, dried flowers

I collected from my summer walks.

The rose petals are burgundy like wine

a shade of burnt yellow that reminds

me of death.

I have them in glass jars from

my empty peanut butter containers

    Royal Doulton saucer cups

    my mother-in-law served cherry sauce in

    glass dishes with Christmas carvings of mistletoe

outside is a windstorm, freezing rain

Christmas Eve chill

but inside the rose petals and lavender leaves

are waiting for me to press them up

against my bookmarks

and turn them into some artsy object

to give away to strangers

or sell for the price of a cup of coffee

I pick them, water them, love them,

groom them, dry them, anticipate

their deterioration, revival

their inferno

as they metamorphosis

into energy

an 1888 painting in France

still life in front of a candle.

SOIL BELOW MY FEET

You choose to let it take you under
      as if you had no hands
      to stop the tsunami in your heart
it is unforgiving
your train never arrived

I will never forgive you
for allowing your shadow
to take over your light

and even your thank you was not authentic

my feet ache from standing

for so many years

waiting for you

to arrive.

I'm sorry you feel that way was the last text I ever sent you.

Now I feel how the earth digs between my toes and never judges.

IX

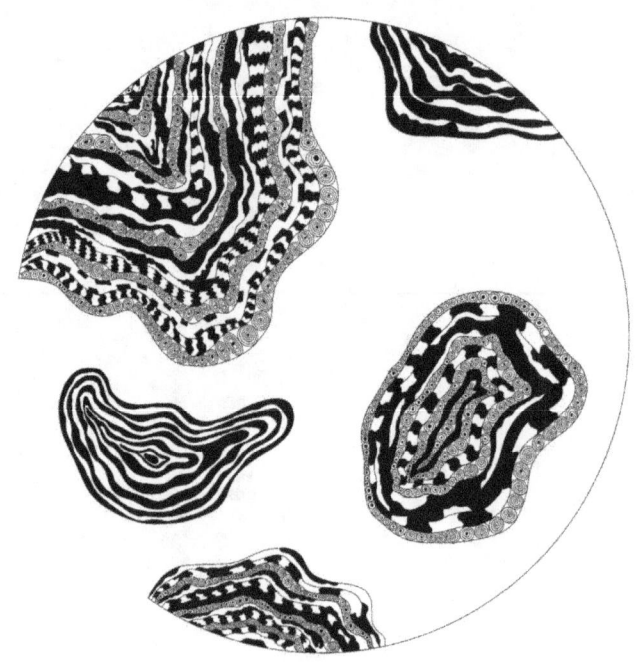

Gaia

PART IX

GAIA

MY SKIN IS GREEN AND BLUE

The caps on my skin

create marks

as humans pass and walk on me

blind to the heat of the sun

my water keeps rising

and soon I will asphyxiate

on gritty sand

tender trees

submerging houses

those greedy humans

who disregard my love

for them

they think I am invincible

the dirty masks on my body

have stained me

of course, I have a heart

it is the earth

of course, I have a mind

it is the sky

of course, I have a soul

it is the water

of course, I have a body

it the fire magma

I cry rain

                I yell thunder.

I shout storms

                I fear pipelines.

I screech hail

                I remember people

with feathers, who loved me.

Let nothing be as it once was.

I vibrate and ache for light

as my wrath seeks justice and karma

I give to humans my cells

they reject and turn them into condos

cities in the seas

billions on fantasies

as governments sink valleys

dehydrate lakes

contaminate oceans

violate laws of nature

swim with their suits on.

I give warnings

wave yellow sirens

use flamingos as SOS

yachts are full of

obscene parties in gold bikinis

floods bare my teeth for millions

who have their eyes closed while awake.

I see you picking up five candy wrappers

one coffee lid

half a broken wheel

you are all alone

no others care at seven a.m.

they throw the coffee cup out the window

I see you

 but destruction whispers

in my ear

It's too late.

I watch you bend and pick up a tie wrap

a water bottle lid

I sigh with you at the brown bag of fast food wrappers

    I send a bird to you to sing *It's too late*

THE SHIFT OF A HISTORICAL AREA

A man alone in the Arctic

Blomstrandbreen Glacier

Melted 104 years apart

Two photos: then vs. now

Proof of reality

Melting ice caps

Images from NASA

1999 vs. 2014

Shrinking Aral Sea in Central Asia

Drying up of the Sea

Makes season change

Thinning glaciers in Muir melt Alaska

Droughts in Arizona and Utah

Snow falling in the Sahara Desert

Bolivia's second largest lake dries up

Poopo Lake

Ice Avalanche in Tibet

Iceland's glaciers slowly melting away

Less ice forming in the Bering Sea

Shrinking glaciers in New Zealand

Beach erosion in Texas

James River floods in South Dakota

Hawaiian island disappears

Desert fires in Australia

Dry conditions

Pools of melting water in Antarctica

Heavy rains flood Peru

I should stop here

Your head is filled with fake news

Climate change does not exist, they say

How can you be fooled by the evidence?

You would rather believe the lies

Than listen to the crying of the planet

How much more proof does humanity need?

IN THE PAST

1.

we roamed with leather on our skin
        feathers in our hair
        nomads written in our cards
ate off the land
rode the horses
as a way of life
  not sport
we spoke to horses before the awakening
we had our own language
        before language existed
we honored silence and past lives
        respected our ancestral land
        which belonged to the rightful owner, Gaia

2.

I was a Mohawk

        and my mother was my dear friend

I was a healer

        and my plants & herbs, my soulmate

everything we were

        we are

everything we seek

        we will find one day in a lifetime

that will be our last

I was a lightworker

        before the word existed.

3.

A man alone

4.

Moments are meant to last

        not cut off with video

words are meant to be listened to

        not ignored to go on TikTok

hearts are lonely brains

        with a DNA to remember all the traumas

        of every life

        of a million years.

Take the sky inside your breath

        let it sweep you off your feet

        like an eternal lover

with a karmic contract that will never abandon you

        no matter how hard you try to

leave.

5.

I did not know that when I gave birth to my children; they were going to change others' lives with music. When I look at their pictures now, they look like twins, when I look at their childhood photos they look like strangers. I called them my little freaks once, and it stuck. Once they were the same colors and had no broken parts together. That is when I knew as I sat in the backseat of the car and their black and gold shirts dazzled me with their star seed. They were deep in the ground once as buds. Now their branches are songs, and their leaves are voices. Now they are Gaia's children.

They came to me because I asked for them.

6.

I write numbers as if there is a beginning and
end
      I write words as if poetry matters.
I meditate
      as if the world will hear me
I cry
      as if I am all alone
I plant herbs and write recipes

       as if no one will burn my witch books

but

  I

    Fear

we will go back to the past

      and they will hunt my name

hang me again

      for being a healer for Gaia.

7.

In the past, we made our ancestors into Gods

legends

    no matter

 their faults

and our women were warriors

        intuitive gifts of knowledge

feminine mystique with strong

   armor in their souls

N O T afraid to say I AM A WOMAN.

8.

it all comes down to this.

    the day my son was born

           the number after six

the third eye   your lucky number   my lucky #

    our lucky number   the time my alarm clock rings

the time the sun sets

  relaxing time

    the tea after dinner

        the opening of the eyes at dawn

the time you have a minute or two

    to think

        about all the things you avoid

        the only way to end a poem

        that never ends.

and the moment I knew I had a daughter

    to create life again.

PANDA

I see your yin and yang colors

surrounded by bamboo shoots

your eyes as delicate as your mother's

your nature as fragile as your father's

I tiptoe on the forest floor

feel the earth between my toes

I know you watch me closely

I see you in my dream

in my reiki healing you say

> *hello I love you*

and I know

to reply

with a smile

for life on earth

is not as it may appear

you are surrounded by fewer trees

less relatives

>   family without breath
>
> a cracking history
>
> >   a flood of furniture
>
> as people sit on your food in fancy chairs and tables
>
> >   you starve for barks
> >
> >   with your arms crossed
> >
> >   your shoulders slumped
>
> the universe needs your guidance, your quietude
>
> >   your resonance
>
> we cannot have you on a list that keeps dying
>
> >   you are my spirit animal
> >
> >   a tender touch
>
> in a greedy mud bank.
>
> You look at me as if you are
>
> >   the last species left
>
> and I spread my arms wide
>
> >   to let your sorrow
> >
> >   fall on my shoulder.

We learn the most about animals

    by looking deep within

        ourselves

I wish you would speak, but I'm afraid to listen.

YANOMAMI WOMAN

My tribe is asleep

The machines are my alarm clock

We come out of our homes

Know that our eyes do not lie

Our ears do not want to hear this ruckus

We only want to walk and cut our herbs

Gather our food

Live our peaceful life off the land

We are over 50,000 people in over 450 villages

The Amazon is our home

On the border between Venezuela and Brazil

I know because I am a healer

I am a woman

You cannot kill all of us.

REMINDERS OF NATURE

Why do people need to be reminded

to walk every day?

Why is it such a chore

        to seep the sun's ray?

Come out from the inside

        bloom, do not hide.

The trees search for your eyes,

        your hugs, your morning rise.

Why did you stop taking photos of the sunset?

        You already know you need a reset.

Take the time to breathe in,

        the air is a constant win.

SPACE X

While we sip this Chardonnay,
billionaires are buying up properties triple the
price to build a city of solar power
with tunnels and no traffic,
no more texting and driving
or motorcycle accidents to cry over.
Let's fly on SpaceX Starship
for seven months
to land on dead land, we cannot breathe on.
Let us take a walk inside a frigid dome
or use the first-floor mudroom
in our new Marsha home,
looks like we live in an egg now:
It's shockproof
cylindrical
spherical,
toroidal.
Let us live in a small space together in space
for months and months,
our bodies adjust to gravity
and we fight daily
because what else is there to do?
When time has no presence here,
waiting on unappetizing food in sealed cans,
exercising in floating gyms.
But wait

when we land on Mars,
it may be -60 degrees Celsius, or worse
you will never walk outdoors again.
No need for bikinis or flip-flops,
there is a dust problem, storms
covering the entire planet.
Under its power,
for the lingering weeks
our well-being can deteriorate,

life support systems collapse, or
we can die of loneliness.

Are you tempted now?

In an underground city,
dust on solar power windows destroying
sunlight, no fresh air,
no ocean, mountains
animals, no trees
only dust, how it threatens our existence,
by 2051
as the mass migration arrives,
we could be smooth-talked
by solar power persuasion,
cleaning dust off the grimy windows,
that will pay you so much money you
never thought capitalism
could tempt like Satan.
All the robots have our menial jobs:
Trash Collection, Barber, Nanny
Sales Clerk, Factory Worker;
AI writes our books now.
Earth is dying of hunger.
Mars is living cosmic radiation.

Are you tempted now?

Never you say while I sip my
Chardonnay, the rich hue of the wine
gold as the grand sky
as the sun sets
over our gilded universe.

X

Love

PART X

LOVE

LOVE

1.

Sun

When I do not see you my heart aches

from all the lack of oxygen

it could be days

without your touch

yet feels like decadent years gone by.

Your warmth breaks down my brick walls

pulls apart all the steel bridges

that took me years to build.

Your eyes on me melts candles

shatters glass

cooks meals

as if the day has finally begun.

We only have a few hours together

always waiting for that time to end

to go back to being another person

we never met.

You only know the side of me that touches

your skin

the one that dashes in and out

of the clouds for a reason

the one who gave you a book

you still hide.

I did not want to find your presence in this poem

your love was an illusion you brought onto me

I believed every word

up until the sun peeked into me

and woke me up

avoiding your growth inside of me

is as impossible as the rays

you distribute to the dying earth.

When I see you

I squint my eyes

my heart used to ache

now it shines.

Our force together is not an image

or a device—

It is a lit candle

attracting the spirits

without knowing its strength.

You and I together

are that flame

in every lifetime

From the one where we died

jumping off the cliff

holding hands

with glitter in our eyes

to this one

where the sun

shimmers on every place

we ever met.

The potency of its potential

filling us with love

the kind you can never hold onto

for the one you can never have

because they are too far

or too high

or too cold

or too unaware

with someone else.

2.

Mercury

The illusion kept growing

        Awards

Gowns with gold sequence

        Nominations

Statures made of Earth's metal

        Select me

        Look at me

Powder rooms with white faces

        Be my fan

Rumors of midnight winds

My hair is falling out

Soft seductive sexy

Poses with 100 filters

Masks for every lens

I write poetry.

Enter at your own risk

Click follow

Memoirs of a lost artist

I live in Bali now

PTSD

Childhood aches

Book Signing event

Smile

3.

Earth

Virgos are grounded. We produce
                        think
                        do
                        act
                        criticize
grow inner rewards
    lose at love
win at work
    lose a part of our seed
          planting
                    working
     organizing
     alphabetical order
     for spice racks
     used books
open up ground

feel my back spikes

    I am a dinosaur now

Open up soil

    take my scattered dust balls

    my carpet banging

    my five unedited manuscripts

    my pens with no more inks

    my father's diary

    dig up my family tree

      I need it.

      Fake a hello—

      Hope no one notices the cracks

      of the mask.

Virgos lie down on silky sand

          Grass

          Leaves

          Branches

Waiting for the sun to come out to love them.

Virgos seem alert, present, focused

then fly off to South America for six months

pretend to be tropical birds

    ancient horses

the faster the animal

    the better for their psyche.

Aries, well, we never had a chance.

Libra is my soul mate.

4.

Venus

I stare at the title of this poem

the way I stared at a comment

a man I used to know

made on Twitter

about my writing

being self-absorbed

he knows what he did

checkmate

game ended.

Venus only exists in fairy tales

playlists, poems, sunsets

all the intangible abstract things

    I keep trying to grasp.

Men are like that, appear one way

then another —

disappear

reappear

with new love letters.

Venus and I

we have a history

of searching for soulmates

the word alone makes us swoon

once upon a time

poems tempted us

songs destroyed us

now we know love is safe

it is a warm blanket on a weeknight

watching NFL Monday night football

it is a three-a.m. wake-up call

to pick up the kids

it is a warm cup of tea on the couch

it is a fight about money being spent

it is a grocery bill

      doctor appointment

vacation

      it is everything you take for granted

and complain about.

When I married, I married for love

      the sand does not slip

it tempts

      you

      to

      be stepped on

      barefoot

      naked

      in secrecy.

Venus is like that

      it keeps your love alive

      and your sex energized

year after year

until the earth

swallows

up

　　　your

　　　fears

and heals your inner child

the pleasure you feel

does not last long

but love remains a rock on a sandy beach

you walk away from for your own good

or collect for memories

or cherish for a lifetime.

5.

Mars

I wrote a poem about you

I called it Space X

Coffin Bell Journal published it.

No one commented on it.

I published it in this book

as an afterthought

Lex and I laughed about Elon Musk

reading it

but nothing happened.

I do not want any part of

your distorted illusion

    living in a cone house

    no air

    no love affairs

I do not like the color red anymore

    too old

      for wolf tricks

I like to be fifty-four and home

      sitting at my writing desk

      with Spunky next to me

my future unspoken.

You attract the wrong people

the dreamers

the narcissists

the ones you keep stalking

you kept every poem

to use for firewood.

It is in your nature

      you kill anyone who comes too close

you dye your hair the wrong color

all the dust you make

      petrifies you

you lost soil in 1196

you do not want it back

you got all you need

the rest is a story you do not believe in.

6.

Jupiter

You are everyone's favorite

people love the "biggest" anything

if they only knew you had eighty moons

    (I know it confuses me)

I would stare at the moon

    more than the sun.

Imagine a world where the moons

    all cast a light on you

and the sun hides.

    It is not luck that draws you to people

It is your empathy, it is how time passes

      way too fast in your timeline.

It is how you love everyone back

      even if they do not deserve it.

7.

Saturn

All the rings around you

      protect you

your colors appear as piano notes

      drum beats

Saturday nights do not exist

      morning walks

all the thoughts you keep trapped

      in gas

have nowhere to go.

      I will not count the moons

your coldness will escape

      no classical music

        no afternoon vibrations

the animals will die

we will all be childless

No more responsibility!

    no running

    away

    from

    yourself

    this time

    you have

    really

    done it.

    Gone

    and

    tried

    to make

    it

on your own

but

blinded

by

the drought

of your ancestors.

8.

Uranus

You never wanted me to change

you mistook my coldness

for love

my love for hate

my change

for better

my originality

for blasphemy.

9.

Neptune

Your love it had me
      entwined in knots
the mystery of your illusive texts
      the trapped silent treatment
      lustful love bombing explosions
      blue ice in your veins
sunglasses in the middle of a rainstorm
paranoia about strangers
inventing backstories

when none were needed

pretending to be a poet

to win a high school competition

pretending to be married, unmarried

divorced

alone

single

annihilated

broken

green envy

      skin so soft

          melted my walls

hand in hand

      unmade bed

         galaxy of poems

      sent

          deleted

      resent

          gone into comets

the intrigue is toxic

      your love is

      as cold as

            Neptune

            cannot

     come back to the

    sun   now

           rotted

           from

           no rays.

10.

Pluto

They say you existed once upon a time. Now they say you do not. The secrets we kept we will both take them to the depth of the universe. Where once we were a tiny love, now we are an empty hole. The distance between us is not merely kilometers, but everything unsaid. Bite my tongue with lies. Swallow my confession with alcohol I no longer drink from. Sins no longer guide us out of reality. We do not exist together and never have. It was a recreation of a fantasy. When I look through a telescope I still see you, but you no longer have my love. Even soulmates can't be together forever. Brief moments in one existence is all that is left.

In the distance,

> when you look up at the sky
>
> you might regret one thing for once
>
> never making my name a star
>
> or you will regret nothing
>
> as you once said to me.
>
> Perhaps I will be the one
>
> filled with a glass of regrets
>
> turned into poems.

Universe

XI

PART XI

UNIVERSE

energy

feeling energy

of light

is not a label

or religion

it is the new consciousness

your fears

stepped on

your love awakened

like a bird's morning call

air

it is not what others tell you

it is how you feel

trust your instincts

you cannot deny the feelings

the abundance of energy

words spurting forth

the cup of tea

the mint garden

the green tomatoes

breathe it in

i saw you for an hour. It was enough

to sustain another sixty years or eighty days

i am going to read the fight club

no romance required

only the universe

a book

and myself

fire

some words get caught in my throat

can only be written down on paper

they overpower silence

restrain me and let me go

to the river by the city

where strangers like us

were once lovers

water

we live in it for nine months

the mercury retrograde is fierce

liberty is learning to swim for the first time

prison is letting go of the world

and letting the chain take you under

it is not pretty on the sand

when love hates you

i am no prophet

i am a mere poet or writer

lighting candles and taking lavender oil baths

cleansing brutes off my body

i drink it every day with lemon or mint

i let it remove all the toxins of the day

cook vegan dishes

family dinners

meat and potatoes

i water my garden

float in it

and see how the lion sun

reflects off my body

once upon a time

it was not so scarce

even with all the oceans meeting

the impending gloom

strikes up my soul

to take off my clothes

and turn into Venus

entering Cyprus.

earth

deep secrets i whisper through poetry

inhale the sky

breathe in the moon

seep in the sun

collect the stones

watch the sunset like a child

this part of the world is still Earth

Greece's magic

under the horizon

a glimpse of gods & goddesses

silently echoing your fears & desires

universe

i trusted you in 1109

when i was a witch

i believed in your remedies

in 1300 when no one else did

i bent backward for

a sprig of sage

in 1568

i wore your trees

as ornaments

in 1987 i wrote a song

for you

no one liked it

in 2000 i kept moving around

from city to city

to find you

in 2022

i let you in with words

Part XII

ENERGY

BETWEEN US

When you read the poem
that is about you, you will
know. My sentences
will fill up your five
senses and I will tell you
the secrets you always
wanted to hear. Between
us is a book of fiction,
it cannot turn into poetry.
Once you made up poems
for me like a fresh pot of
coffee. You would exercise
and write me a poem.
Between us are all these
millions of words
deleted. This dead energy
cannot be reborn like a still

born child. That is our love,

we never had a chance to live in it

for longer than a few stolen hours.

All the energy we made together

has become someone else's breath.

SNOW

We hibernate like grizzly bears

we make homemade chicken soup

we heal our unforgiving childhood

but when the snowstorm starts

I go outside for a walk at night

and the delicate quiet

cures my water dripping trauma

the holograph serenity

calms my nervous system

the bleak snow

wets my hair

reddens my cheeks

my feet and hands

turn yellow quickly

I learn to turn a ten-minute walk

into a two-hour wave

the Raynaud's disease

does not mean I should flee

only that I am learning to live

a new normal

in the country turned city.

I am allergic to the cold

the winter frosts

the solid ice

the frozen peas

yet here I am

sticking out my tongue

letting each flake revive me

like a defibrillator

delivering shock

to a heart attack

in the middle of the night

and all you can do

is look at death straight on

until the spring.

Nature likes to hide itself.

- Heraclitus

Searching for water in a forest is a survivor game – take my glasses off, I like lonely people

they remind me of trees.

I LIKE LONELY PEOPLE

    they remind me of trees

    the way

    their stillness

    draws you

    inside their bark

I like lonely people

    they remind me of raindrops

    the way

    they all meet

    at the bottom of a well.

I like lonely people

    they remind me of a popular song

    the lyrics

    we listen to alone and cry in the car

    searching for a tissue.

I like lonely people

    they remind me of a burning house

    the one you drive by

    thanking God

    it was not your books on fire.

I like lonely people

    they remind me of all the versions of myself

    the one who slept through important events

    the one who arrived first at a party

    the one who missed her graduation

    the one who sits alone at a café

    the one who thought love only happens once

    the one who prefers trees to voices

    the one who needs eros

            agape

            touch

and pretends not to.

ODE TO THE LANDFILL

It is something I do not like to research

the leftover images

//

my food boils in my stomach

//

I throw the wrapper from my chocolate under my desk

inside my flowered trash bin

//

I have two pens with no ink

a piece of paper with lists

crumbled wrappers

tissue paper

Christmas napkins

popcorn bag

salt & vinegar bag

lined paper with to-do lists

//

Was there ever a time it was not important?

the trash is forty percent paper

paper, yes paper —

sitting there cross legged

looking back at you

with memoirs to tell

no pens to write on

while the storks sit on top

of a landfill in Guwahati

and pose for a National Geographic snapshot

//

there is a layer of soil

upon another layer

decomposing process

    //

emitting methane

        greenhouse gas

climate change

//

toxins

(how poetic is to write a poem about the way no one cares as much as they think they do)

better to take out the trash every Monday morning

until the following week

it hurts too much

to feel it all

to know it all

//

for people like us

//

who see through paper

and have broken glass as hearts.

THE NATURE OF HER HANDS

Lines up and down, sideways, zig zags

protruding veins

with no nail polish

one wedding band —

gold

from 1960.

You can tell it was only washed

at the sink

with Palmolive soap

with loving care

and never at a jeweler's.

She is planting her tomatoes

one by one

side by side

in case they need company

or silence

in Bali, the lights are out

in the middle of the day

does she want to plant

      or run to a new land

      of lightness?

I ask her, "Do you love your tomatoes?"

She squints at me, the sun blocking her view

"They grow when you love them," she answers.

ONE AMONG MANY

One stork on a rock

with his family

overlooking the layers of trash

hoping to find food

where none exist.

Where is the water?

Where are the newborns?

I have traveled so far

to find this

tragedy in the pink day.

She looks at her mother

who is crying

for humanity

she looks at her father

who is planning

a route out of here

she looks at her cousins

who shout *let's fly away.*

She wants to sit there for a while

she observes the human

with the camera

snapping photos

of her and her family.

She does not pose

      nor smile

she looks away

      her profile is more direct

she knows they will look

at her family as the same

      but they are not the same at all

      she has blue eyes

      her brother Sean has green eyes

her parents adopted her

      they never leave anyone behind

it is a photo

   and she is the main star

she stands out

her profile is classic.

She takes after the Ancient Storks

   they were wise

   understood truth and beauty

   ancient and modern civilizations are one

   they understood every living entity

they did not need definitions

nor establishments.

SIX STONES FROM A BEACH

1.

You have horizontal lines of a brown semblance

your shape is flat on the bottom

with a round right curve

on top

almost as if

a slight tilt to the right

and an opening on the bottom

could have turned you

into a heart.

2.

I am light brown

a left sided heart

imperfections

loveless

abandoned

everyone who picked me up

threw me back in the water

except for you.

You saw my awkwardness

and saved me.

3.

She is triangle with scars

they have poked her

raped her

abused her

stabbed her

she is light cream

with tan scars

you touch her skin

and she cries

you can feel her history

sing tragic sad songs

if you look closely

you will see the cross

others will tell you

that is not a cross

    it is a plus sign

but you know

your instincts know

the moment you picked her up

you saw through her eyes.

4.

He is a sandy square

with one dark wound

some white marks.

He was around when Jesus

walked the Earth

he saw the miracles

but could not speak.

5.

I am the color of

cashew

the shape of a mountain

a dinosaur tooth

smooth

when you touch me

you can see an alien

your skin will tingle

goosebumps

visions

dreams

put me back

with my five friends

do not even think of stealing me

from this beach.

6.

She is pearly, creamy

off-white love

with light sandy eyes

caught between shapes

Is she a circle?

square

rectangle

Why this need to label?

She needs light

      sun

      love

      company

to love her

cherish her and she will notice

when you look away

she likes to be with her five friends

    on a shelf

    of a writing desk

    to be touched

    neglected

    reminded

    obscure

    abstract

    tangible

    invited.

NO

I say no to alcohol

it can burn your soul

with evil eyes

take you out of a memory

recreate it

or even worse

forget it ever happened.

Until one day

ten years later

you remember everything.

One glass can lead to another

you turn into the adaptation of yourself

you locked up behind prison bars

you want that history

to bloom in the snow

under harsh winds, smog,

and unbearable coldness

I say no to alcohol

to free all the clones of myself

to walk in a path with my initials

    on a tree trunk

to be an adult

    with a child's innocence

free to be the authentic core

without the enemy in my blood

whispering to do all those things

I should not

remembering all the moments

I tried so hard to forget

breathing the air without fear

not picking up alcohol's partner

in my lungs

to keep the liquid company

my nervous system has had enough

of these glamorous lies of kings

who need to create art

to be someone.

Going back to the beginning

with no pesticides

fertilizer in my blood

to fog up my vision.

Pure and uninhibited me

maybe a little dull

but new renditions break free

to shout, Yes

    I'll have green tea

        while everyone else drinks wine.

THE BIKE PATH

It took me forty-five minutes

to drive to a lake up north

and the same amount of time

to feed the concrete

under my running shoes

following a dotted yellow line

with arrows

no one followed.

A young girl and her dad

swing by me

ringing their bell

flowers peek out of concrete fences

I try to name them in my head

I get dandelions

the first flower children

give to teachers to show their love.

Only a five-minute walk from my house

and the air appears like a fresh bowl of fruit

it is complimentary

a costless love

we overlook

a young woman speed walks

a couple promenades

a family strolls by

I avoid eye contact

walk toward a soaring tree

I stop

I want to hug it

it whispers to me

    who cares what people think

I touch the tree with both my hands

    close my eyes

the trunk is a rush of red electrical currents

and a purple light

I hear the tree talking to me

I hear people staring at me

my senses are alert

Bocelli created music

with no eyesight

my third eye

activates. It feels as if a garden

has bloomed in my mind in ten seconds

I do not know how long I stand there

when I open my eyes

I release a version of myself

I no longer want.

XIII

Habitats

Part XIII

HABITATS

MOJAVE DESERT

You try not to slip on ice

you walk methodically —

breaking a leg is the last thing you

need right now.

Yet the moment your feet

walk in the desert

all you want to do

is go under the gold

as if there is a secret

under all those soft-spoken grains

and you want to put your ear

down to the ground

as Sexton advises

but the ground

is not supposed to be wobbly

yet here you are

walking in the rain shadow of the Sierra Nevada

Mountains

your great great grandmother in your past life

was born in this desert

your friend Adelina

was your mom

you both walked barefoot

and kissed your lovers goodbye

as if they would come back

from the dead

with all the answers

the desert keeps.

THE AMAZON

The best love affair

is the one you have

with yourself. That

time you wake up and

decide you want to go

deep deep into the

Amazon rainforest

where no friends

of yours would

dream of going.

It's not Cannes here

or the south of

France with Gucci

purses. It's survival

of the love you

have for yourself.

The one you want

to keep watering.

The one who carries

a pen in her purse

in case she needs

to write on a

napkin —

Or even her hand

anywhere but the phone.

The dream of

waking up to a heavy

rainfall

surrounded by

sloths, gorillas,

blue butterflies,

jaguars, tree frogs,

iguanas, macaws,

deciding which

canopy can hold

you up the best.

Loving yourself

is an art —

The art of giving up

all the clothes on

your back

to step naked

into the jungle —

Fearless,

in love with your own

naked skin

for once

and tired of covering it up.

It is time for another one

of your rebirths

in the middle of the heart

of the rainforest —

Where you may

never be seen again

or come out the same way

with new layers

you never knew

you even had.

POLAR

A white blanket on the top and the bottom

of our world

{How can any human survive

in these extreme cold temperatures}

we are in our heated homes

with fuzzy slippers

eating skinny popcorn

counting calories

waiting for summer

like a squirrel for nuts.

The permafrost has no time

for trees sprouting

warm bikini days

even if the sun is out

for twenty-four hours

you are still ice cold.

Do you want to visit me there?

No, I'd rather stay on this couch

    watching football

    eating ice cream

    weighing myself

    every twenty-four hours

    naked, before breakfast

    because the ice

    cannot penetrate

    the broken heart

    of the Earth.

TUNDRA

I see no climbing trees

cotton snow of quilts

frozen soil all year

turns to ponds

in the summer

the wind knots my hair

dries my wrinkles

the lack of rain

fills my eyes with tears

      I see you

tiny plant

Hello there

you bloom in the worst

conditions

you are resilient

like my daughter

who has weathered all the storms

inside her

and comes out a survivor

shedding old skin

with every rebirth.

I see colorful rushes

purple sedges

yellow birches

blue dwarf heath

cotton grass

indigo dryland sedges

golden sphagnum moss

magenta crustose

the type of vegetation

    you do not care to photograph

yet the toughest

    is not always the prettiest to look at

I see a blue butterfly

    watch if fly off

    riding all her trauma

leaving it behind the moss

for good

unable to bloom in this landscape

but vigorous enough to find a new one.

EVERGREEN FORESTS

Here you will not find

a shower of old leaves

on the ground to crunch on

with your Nike running shoes

no rejected leaves to observe

the constant love

of its leaf

for its tree

and no loss of time apart

or even loneliness

to search for company

or waiting for the next season

to unfold like a crumbled paper

you never meant to throw out.

Here you will find

an inner warmth

from the inside of your soul

located all around the globe

spin the world

in your living room

in front of a fireplace

you will find me

patient

unchanged

familiar

from the last time you drove by me

on your way to New York City.

Do not chop me down

do not decorate me with blue lights

do not place your gifts

under my branches

I was not meant to be in your house.

You may like the pine smell of my skin

but there is more to me

than height

why are you paying sixty-dollars

for me when I am free?

No one owns me

you are fooled again

by the world

creating price tags

on nature

I am a free spirit

please do

    not

    change me

    into fabrications of your illusions.

SEASONAL FORESTS

Fauna & Flora
    bless the Goddesses of fertility and the flower
Africa
    humid hotspots with no internet Asia
    agriculture destruction with no morals
Pacific Regions
    rainfall cleanses the annihilation of the lost souls
Central America
    converted into pastures for money South America
    do not vanish — please save all our lives
Deciduous
    your four seasons are an example of our future survival rate
Semi-evergreen
    you lose parts of yourself but not the whole
Monsoon
    your sighs build crops Rainfall
    your tears stitches cracks Wet season
    without your anger we would not find peace
Savannah
    one open canopy in the part of the world humans are not meant to dwell.

GRASSLANDS

As tall as the trees

You may find me hidden

Surrounded by the greenery

Some sedge and rush

Around my dangerous yet delicate edges

To secure me from human eyes

If you look close enough

You would be surprised

To smell some clover

And other medicinal herbs

Around my shrubbery

We dominate planet Earth

And without us

How would you breathe?

You pretend not to notice me

While riding the subway

Although you cannot see me

In your city life

You think of me often

Perhaps dream of how soothing

I made your life

Once upon a time.

THALASSA

I speak Greek to you

to teach you

the language of my ancestors —

I want you to speak to me

in my language

I want you to hold the waves for me

let me step on water for you

    your surface warms me

    gaslights me

no matter what cliché I may write —

    you know every poem is about you

    even when I deny it.

Oceans are like lovers

lonely when apart

full when together.

REIKI

I watched a terrible movie

with A actors

making fun of Reiki

but promoting fashion brands

and racism

I could not take more than

fifteen minutes

the veil has been lifted

I can read through scripts

notice the bullshit narrative

shake my head

at all the name drops

cameos

feel the fake acting

making my skin crawl

when will everyone wake up?

They want you exactly

where you are

scrolling

not thinking

paying for everything

that is free

tying you to therapists

laughing at

    "energy therapy"

    as if the joke is on you

wake up Jim Morrison said

over 30 years ago

and still, no one is listening.

FACTS

The science is not only for scientists

the facts you cannot refute

    the sun gives the Earth its energy

let it heal you

    the sun is Earth's primary source of life

allow it to be yours

    the moon is Earth's natural satellite

follow its guide

the path is in phases

Oxygen is produced and released by trees

stay close to their breath

must I go on with the science

to understand the energy

you feel now.

A STORY

When you let down your guard

stop watching the news

tell yourself

it's a *narrative*

look within yourself

and say —

"I want to create

my story. I will

not set my alarm.

Let my body wake me

up with the sun.

I want to follow

the moon at night

while I take a

walk. I won't

fear the night

because they

tell me it's
dangerous. I
won't fear being
alone in a city
because they
tell me I'll be
kidnapped. I
won't fear people
because they tell
me I should."
It's a story you're living
without paper.
Buying a journal
writing it down
makes it yours.
No copies for
the internet
no sharing on
a computer.

One copy of your

journal

your poems

your notes

for you to do

with them

what you will.

To write them

in a letter,

to save

them for your

children,

to burn them

to collect them

to publish them

to reread them —

to sit under a tree

with them

the sun in the day

under the moon at night

to let vitality

fuel your words

to let the Universe

understand your agony.

    It's your story to share

    no one can plagiarize it

    or retell it

    like you can.

SOLAR ENERGY

Your warmth makes my living room alive

with written invitations

to sit down and bask in your presence

You have the capacity

of being everywhere

and nowhere

we can see you

      but cannot touch you

we take advantage of your strength

and suck up all your weaknesses

humanity has mistreated your elegance

we used to worship you

with fewer men and women

in gardens and forests

living directly under your eyes

now we hide from you

protect our skin

from the damage we created

build homes with your never-ending love

you keep forgiving our mistakes

but our time is running out

and so is your generosity

every living element has an ending

we have kept using you

abusing you

polluting you

kissing you with lies

lying to you with laws

abandoning you

you do not call it revenge

because it is not

the right word —

it is Karma

although overused like sunscreen

on old, wrinkled skin

it has the zeal

      you cannot see

      but only feel

      the science they neglected to teach you in school.

DEAR GAIA

1.

Gaia thought she had a four-hundred-page book of poems to share with you

and me as her vessel.

The journal I wrote all these poems on is almost at an end

but my poems continue like rain

Gaia has so much to tell you

she says it

for the ones who cannot feel her verve

and the ones who can

open up your third eye

the one that has been with you

since the beginning of your time

who knows when that was

do you think Darwin did? Is his

truth the smartest of the two

they've sold you? Is Adam and Eve

a better fairytale?

Both written by men

perhaps Gaia needs a pen too —

      She speaks a lexicon

only a few can understand

she does not care about Adam, God, Allah,

Jesus, wellness coaches, influencers,

politicians, teachers, priests,

she has no name

you can call her the Source

if that is what your word of the day is

Virginia Woolf wrote

"For most of History, Anonymous was a woman."

I would say

"For most of History, Gaia was a woman oppressed."

Take that sentence and fill in the blanks

do with it what you will

we need to keep Gaia as free

as she is

live with her and respect her

I talk to her and say

"Gaia, I love you. Thank you."

Other times, I remain silent

say nothing

write nothing

 exist

as she does.

2.

Dear Gaia,

    More people should write you love letters while listening to elegant jazz on a Monday morning. When you suggest to people they should buy a journal and write, they think, "I can't write." "I'm not a writer."

Billions of people talk to you every day. You listen to them and you reply in the shape of a rain cloud, or the sun shining after a storm

>or coins found in snowbanks

>or address numbers

>or price tags

>total amounts of bills

"Everyone can write in a journal. Nothing has to be shared." You whisper in the wind.

>You love words and may respond with music.

"Do not be so hard on yourself."

>You adore our wondrous sounds

More people ask to reach out to you

Treat you as a friend

>A confident

>A wise sage with owl eyes

Thank you for listening to me when everyone else looks at their phone for validation.

3.

All the artistry

    Comes in threes

All the pyramidical faith

    Arrives in trinities

Not talking about worshipping men

    Or saints on a painted wall

You can rename yourself

    Baptize your soul

    Any name you want

Convince the public

    You are immortal with a red dress

    A God of art, music, poetry, philosophy

    Finance, crypto, greed, lies

Whatever you fancy

Nowadays, money matters

While earth shatters

Gaia seeps into tea leaves

Ready to be absorbed in your body

Are you ready to receive her or deceive her?

ROTATION OF THE EARTH

I am turning counterclockwise

I meet my surface in the North Pole

and in the South Pole

like a child meets their parents

after a day of separation

in twenty-four hours

I make the sea level rise

day turns to night

all because of the stamina

of the sun and the moon

      between me

my mother

      and my father

my mother

 the mythical moon

my father

the spiritual sun

and I

    its child

trapped in its intergenerational trauma.

REVOLUTION

Half the Earth faces the rays of my father

while the other half sleeps in the arms of my daughter

my body sways to the music

        from east to west

        from left to right

my father wakes up early every day

sleeps late at night

like yours does

his secrets remain trapped in volcanoes

I can hear my mother crying

under the light of her mother

but she is a queen and never betrays her man

she makes him see the light in the winter

kisses the darkness in the summer

I am the revolution

we are immortal people

I am slowly running out of strength

my parents are weaker

my children are planning to kill me

I am waiting for *your* revolution

to go back to my womb.

LOVE LETTERS

I stopped writing love letters

I am writing to Mother Earth now

Happy V-day to you, Gaia

and your abundance of love

    you give us naturally

we do not have to bargain for it

or lie for it

or orchestrate

or put up black masks

we accept you like a morning forget-me-not flower

    neglect you

    like the elders

    when true love dies

    we wish to go back in time

to write love letters

instead of yelling about the trash

or the clogged sink.

I stopped writing love letters to me

because no one deserved my love again

I thought they did

but they never knew

or believed I could love them back

as if I was a waterfall

they could not tell

my love poured out

unwillingly

I could not stop it

no matter what darts

burnt my heart.

Now I write to you, Gaia

and know you listen

more than any lover.

You are my one true love.

I thought it was a man.

Later, I thought it was poetry.

I know it is you, Gaia.

This book is for you.

I love you.

BIRTHDAY

Rivers floating with balloons
      plastic colorful straws
     stained party hats
    pink streamers
Earth's birthday is not once a year

watching videos of people

cleaning rivers

sharing them

means nothing

since when did doing nothing mean something

you share it in a story

who is feeding you these lies

Are you a better human now?

Have you saved the earth by thinking you are doing something?

Break free of the rules and create your own story

you are your own judge and jury

oversharing traumatic stories

scrolling death on the screen

only makes you feel numb

birthdays come once a year

but life is celebrated every day

in real life with real people

with real events

that most of the time

you keep to yourself.

RADIOACTIVE DECAY

The internal heat makes her tears pour out

        her potassium levels are too high

She had to take another blood test

        her uranium

        thorium

are breaking down

she keeps releasing steam

but her internal organs

hold so much coffee grains

she keeps painting eyes on trees

no one can see

and still her cup

is nearly empty

who will refill the crust?

The mantle sheds its color

He watches from above

His eyes and hands trying

to hold down the chariot

while the inevitable heat from the decayed organs

slows the cooling of her skin —

Who will be able to breathe

    on top of a mountain

when she cannot sustain our neglect?

IN SICKNESS

We are married to the Earth

In sickness and in health

We may not have had a ceremony

But our souls are unified

      From the reishi mushroom

      To the ginger tales

      And the mint gardens

      As brittle wildflowers

      We sprout from concrete.

MIRACLES

The miracle is you

remember when Jesus turned water into wine at a wedding you attended in a past life

your soul recalls everything

scientists theorize

    argue

    that Earth made it here by luck

    faith vs. luck

    right vs. wrong

    fact vs. truth

What does your soul tell you?

When did you stop listening?

I read an article about life on Earth and maybe we are here by chance

nothing truly makes sense

the Theory of Evolution is so outdated and taught over again as if it is a Bible

the complete opposite of what it represents

    what about the Great Pyramids and the Sphinx

    the miracle of the Sun —

    thousands witness their clothes wet, then dry in seconds

it was Lourdes —

The grotto healing people by drinking and bathing it

A woman who came back to life

after having no pulse for 45 minutes

a boy who fell into an icy stream

resuscitated after two hours of CPR

The miracle is you —

It is all around you

No one has the answer to your question

stop asking google

you already know

your soul answers

you need to start believing

more in miracles

and less in journalism.

XIV
Internal Earthquakes

Part XIV

INTERNAL EARTHQUAKES

Dear Diary, Feb. 21, 2023

I had my first earthquake in a car. My shoes and socks got soaked in a Tupperware filled with rapini and tomato sauce. Stuck between my dad driving and my mom hugging me. Three people in the front seat and four people in the back were the norm. Seatbelts were ornaments.

In 2013, I owned a daycare. It was the day after Remembrance Day, I was doing my office work, answering emails, and listening to Blondie's song, "Heart of Glass."

At 2:15 in the afternoon, I heard a loud bang. I looked up, thinking a plane had landed on the roof. For a split second, I did not know what was going on at all. I looked at the small window on my door and saw a teacher with horror written on her face. As soon as I ran out my office door, my eyes played tricks on me.

A car crashed into my daycare, going through the glass windows and landing on the wall that separated my business from my neighbor's.

Suddenly, men surrounded the car and lifted it together. They turned into earth angels. I went under the car and the wheel as if it was the easiest step in the world. I placed the length of my arm under the squashed face of a head that was under a tire, and lifted a tiny body on one arm as if I was superwoman. I placed her gently on a mat and did CPR.

Her body was blue, and I kept thinking, *please live, please live,* as I blew air into her lungs. *Please live.* These must have been the longest breaths I ever gave to anyone. I never thought I would be on my knees over the blue body of a tiny three-year-old girl praying for her life.

Lucie, my colleague, was next to me. She had her hand on the little girl's chest, waiting for a breath.

"She's breathing," she finally said.

I looked up at her and sighed. I believed in angels before, but on that day, I had proof.

Someone told me later I was one of those angels.

We were many that day.

I saved a life of a child.

There's an earthquake in my soul

And a volcano of hope in my heart.

I went to her house with a gift when she turned four years old.

Earthquakes happen when the heart can only take so much abuse from the ones who claim to love them.

Volcanoes erupt because hope is denied.

Inside my mind is a universe of lost galaxies trying to find a way out.

Did you ever feel like you were trapped in your life and upset at yourself for giving away your power to those who keep taking it?

Candles emit dreams.

When the car crashed into my world, I started to see through people.

The earth dances when we sing together.

Some souls meet in the middle of the earth to shiver & break glass once in a lifetime.

Fire is like a mad love affair —

    It can heat up your loins with desire, capture your illusion with flames, and take you to cities you can't spell.

How the earth hears our howls from heaven.

God told me about the Source and the Source told me about God.   Apparently, the Universe speaks through secrets you whisper or think about.   One second you are thinking about your ex-lover, the next day, you run into him.   *If* there's a God, *if* there's a Source, they say.

    If there's an ex-lover.

    If. If. If.

If you even exist.

No one has proof of anything.

It is not proof we need   but   Faith.

I see purple and yellow when I close my eyes swirling into a flower while the flame of the candle on my desk sways as fast as the January wind and I try to understand the language of ghosts.

If you feel yourself turn into an angel it means you saved a life.

I quit drinking, smoking, but never loving you. That's why this book is about her. She never lets me be manipulated. She hides behind no mask. Her ground is soî, hard, natural. She opens portals for me. My feet are sore from walking. She accepts my every way. Her love is unconditional. Mother Earth, She is everyone's mother.

Everyone feels earthquakes. The ground swallowing you whole. Trapped with a broken heart inside the crust of colors. Never to finish your untold story. Your contract is up on your way to the grocery store. Everyone fears being caught in a lie.

If only people can see your internal earthquakes, they would know what a brave warrior you are. Your job would not matter, your mental illness would disintegrate into the past, but what matters most are the eyes looking at you in the mirror. Where future, past, present collide inside you and make you whole. Turn you into the mist in the mountains. When you open up your mouth and let out all your crumbled debris, know this: Mother Earth is crying with you, alongside you, beside you, above you, through you, inside you.

You're never alone when you have the Universe inside you, stepping on history, paving a new essence, creating a fragrance from your soul — only you know the ingredients inside.

We need to hold hands with everyone who sees through trees.

If you water yourself, you will grow.

The aftershock of surviving your storm turns the nature of love toward you.

If you don't plant a seed, it will not grow.

Every book comes from paper, which comes from trees, which comes from you, Gaia.

Epilogue

EPILOGUE

1.

The sound of you is in me from the first moment

You created a playlist

To the golden galaxies

Of my handwriting

I burned a poem for you

Gave it to you as a gift

The ashes were never found.

2.

When I caught a frog

        In your room

Under your lamp

I put it in a shoe box

Walked outside

And let it jump down the stairs

Most of the real-life stories

Turn into fantasy.

3.

My bird died

Me and the kids brought Buddy to a vet

They said he had a heart attack.

I cried for my dad

It was less than six months

The bird turned into my father and I cried all the way home

Driving on the highway

Me and the kids buried the bird in the forest

They were only seven and nine years old

But they knew that death is something we cherish

Now the forest is a school.

4.

Children are the healers.

5.

A life without a miracle is not a life.

6.

You should pick up every coin

Read every address

See the balance of your life

You could learn everything from children

If you listen

Instead of correct.

7.

Mothers and Trees are the same. They give until they die.

8.

If you look at an icicle close enough, you will see no future.
Children like to lick them

      break them

            hide them in their pocket

                  poke their friends

and we walk by an icicle forgetting its intrigue.

9.

Look at the leaves through the eyes of a child

Make a wax crayon collage

Touch the snow

Throw the snow in the air

Eat the snow

Lick the snow

Throw it on a friend's face —

We shovel it

As if it will ever stop falling.

10.

Every season teaches you how to love yourself

differently — How to be lonely, friendly, pretty, creative, joyful, sad, empty, happy, full. To live through all four is a gift from the universe. Ribbons, the ocean, and the sky a bow.

11.

The portals are real and not a video game. Art mimics life.

12.

Some people are robots. It's not your responsibility to change them. You have your hands turning into vines with your overgrown soul. Work on your own tangerine turmoil, feed your apple blossom soul, plow your peachy earth to keep sprouting a rebirth of seeds. Live in abundance to care less about frown lines and more about tree lines.

13.

all the lines on your face cannot be erased each one has a
story to tell why hide the truth   stories need to be shared
lines need to be faced every six months lavender plant
grows and you hide your scent sometimes punctuation
stops the roots from touching the sky

14.

Lift your veil to see how mothers love unconditionally and earth is the strongest woman you know with heartbreaking stories and our father the sun keeps poking in and out of her love

take off your mask   open your eyes   let shame rewrite another story without your name   you no longer want to be a part of that flowing river   you want to be reborn you died so many times yet your pot has drops of water the source does not give up   ever

Can you see better now? Throw away your glasses   does your heart ache less?   Do you understand the power you have or are you meant to   meant to   meant to   listen to the sounds   create your own song   even if you cannot read musical notes   or play   let Gaia sing to you her new album.

15.

From now on, until my last breath, I promise to never take advantage of your abundance of love ever again.

16.

When the loneliness lights my candle with its worry, I will blow it out with my powerful breath.

17.

My love for you is as fruitful as a farmer's market on the first day of its crop.

18.

I give myself to the Universe and all of its secrets I hear. I give myself to the motions of a compass to get lost within the center of its core. I give myself to the pink forest in my mind from my childhood where I saw angels on a mountaintop and never doubted their existence.

19.

I listen to the voice of inanimate objects and feel their years of neglect, like a marriage that died a long time ago.

20.

For once and for all
> Let time pass you by
> Without looking at reminders of numbers
> And where you should not be
> But where you are right now.

21.

Promises are not meant to be spoken. You should be able to read my mind by now.

22.

A new version of me is peeling off the layers with every full moon. Art is the moon chasing me from the facade.

23.

My mother is my tree. My father is my earth. My children are my branches. I am the trunk.

24.

The soul has a story for an orchestra to play.

25.

Time is never felt between soulmates of the Earth and the Sun.

26.

Gaia hopes you will respect her soul as much as she does yours.

27.

Every living entity has a delicate soul
a heartbreaking story
and a triumphant rebirth.

Thank you for reading. May the love of Gaia guide you.

ACKNOWLEDGMENTS

Self-publishing this book has been one of the most exciting books to create; from inception to creation, it has been an inspirational journey.

Thank you to Suzi, who helped me format this book and understanding my vision.

Thank you Cynthia De Gregorio for the thematic intricacy of the book cover and her creative illustrations and deep understanding of my vision.

Thank you Maria Papadimitriou for her symbolic illustrations inspired by my poems.

This poetry book is the last of my trilogy, *Love & Vodka* (2016), *Love & Metaxa* (2021), and now *love & gaia*. I did not have an intention of writing a trilogy when I first wrote *Love & Vodka*, but somewhere along the line, it all evolved.

The titles of my last books are linked to alcohol because of my relationship with drinking.

This past year I stopped drinking alcohol. It was as if my soul had just said *Enough*. Enough of this poison inside you. Enough of not knowing what you are doing when you are drinking. Enough not being your true self. Not that I will not drink alcohol ever again. I do not want it to be inside my nervous system, causing me havoc, and turning me into someone I don't recognize.

I want to be free of its toxins in order to control *how* they affect me. I want to be my authentic self. I don't want to rely on alcohol to feel good or bad. Most people have a distinct relationship with alcohol. It surrounds us on a daily basis.

I wrote two poetry books with the titles Vodka and Metaxa, hence my relationship with alcohol has been an intense one throughout my life. For this reason, it inspired me to write a poetry book to end my trilogy on a different beat. When I first tried alcohol at fourteen and got drunk at a party, I knew it was destructive, but I never let go of it until forty years later. I thought it had no control over me. I was wrong. It had *too much* control.

I am a poet. I write what I feel. This book came about quickly and the vivacity to write it was a spark in me that I could not suppress. The shift in the energy field and the universe is real. What would have taken me years to write, I wrote in five months, and here it is, released into the world.

I did not send any poems out for publication. I wanted all these poems to be a complete surprise. The only poem that I added right before I finished my last edits was "Space X." I had written it for another poetry book, but I felt it went better with the theme of this book.

Thank you to *Coffin Bell Journal* for publishing "Space X" on the first day of January, 2023.

I did not want to wait years to publish this book. I felt this had to be now. The urgency to heal Gaia is upon us.

I want this experience between me and you to have no messengers. My voice straight to you, with no editors. I am the writer and editor.

I want to thank Alexandra Meehan who helped me become the poet I am today. Without her editing in *Love & Metaxa*, I would never have developed into the poet I am today.

I hope you take your time with these poems. I hope they resonate with you.

I wrote all these poems by hand in my journal. Since I did my own edits, the poems are not that different from the original. I feel as if my higher self was the one who wrote these poems, and I kept them as raw and authentic as I could.

I want to give a special thank you to my family, Greg, John, Maria, and my mom, Angeliki, for always supporting my writing.

Special thank you to my father, Peter, who has guided me throughout his life and death.

If you would like to send me a personal letter, you can email me at christinastrigasauthor@gmail.com

If you want to write a letter to Gaia, I will accept those as well. I have a template at the back of this book. You can fill it out, snap a photo and send it to me. Let us write letters and love to our Mother Earth.

Write a poem, write a note, write whatever you want. Gaia is listening. She needs us to return her favors.

I love you

Christina Strigas

IMAGE CREDITS

Cover Art

love & gaia by Cynthia De Gregorio

p. 11   *Trees* by Cynthia De Gregorio

p. 15   *Tree of Knowledge* by Maria Papadimitriou

p. 19   *Orange Leaves* by Maria Papadimitriou

p. 47   *Sky* by Cynthia De Gregorio

p. 51   *Full Moon* by Maria Papadimitriou

p. 83   *Ocean* by Cynthia De Gregorio

p. 95   *River* by Maria Papadimitriou

p. 117 *Soil* by Cynthia De Gregorio

p. 125 *gases* by Maria Papadimitriou

p. 135 *Tea* by Cynthia De Gregorio

p. 137 *Tea Leaves* by Maria Papadimitriou

p. 161 *Coffee Beans* by Cynthia De Gregorio

P. 171 *Coffeehouse* by Maria Papadimitriou

p. 181 *Herbs* by Cynthia De Gregorio

p. 187 *Lavender* by Maria Papadimitriou

p. 197 *Seeds* by Cynthia De Gregorio

p. 205 *Petals* by Maria Papadimitriou

p. 219 *Gaia* by Cynthia De Gregorio

p. 227 *In the Past* by Maria Papadimitriou

p. 241 *Love* by Cynthia De Gregorio

p. 267 *Universe* by Cynthia De Gregorio

p. 277 *Energy* by Cynthia De Gregorio

p. 307 *Habitats* by Cynthia De Gregorio

p. 383 *Epilogue* by Cynthia De Gregorio

ABOUT THE AUTHOR

Christina Strigas was born and raised in Montreal, Quebec.

This is her seventh poetry book.

She is Greek-Canadian and proud of her heritage. She is a public school teacher and a part-time Course Lecturer for McGill University.

Please leave a review on Goodreads, Amazon, or any other online site to help spread the word of *love & gaia*. As an indie author your word of mouth helps this book fall into numerous hands, and be read from people all over Mother Earth.

WRITE YOUR LETTER & SHARE IT WITH ME

Date: _____

Dear Gaia,

_____
_____
_____
_____
_____
_____
_____
_____
_____
_____
_____
_____

With Love,

_____

x

www.ingramcontent.com/pod-product-compliance
Lightning Source LLC
Chambersburg PA
CBHW070417010526
44118CB00014B/1797